Teatime Celebrations

Patricia Gentry
Author

Jane Horn
Editor

Craig Mohr
Principal Photographer

Ed Carey
Cover Photographer

Patricia Gentry
Marilyn Smith
Karen Hazarian
Stylists

101
Productions

To the memory of Susan, a beautifully spirited lady, sister, and friend. I dedicate this book to the special celebrations of life and the many times we shared.

Acknowledgments

I would like to express my appreciation to my good friend and cooking assistant Marilyn Smith for her many contributions to this book, in particular for her food styling.

I also want to thank Tina Carter; Edna and Bob Clark; Sarah Clark; Florence Coutts; Nancy Elkins; Mary Ann Evans; Las Fortunas Auxiliary of Assistance League of Santa Monica; Larry, Tracy, and Mark Gentry; Jann Gray; Marylou and Victor Harbaugh; Jane Horn; Susan Jory; Dee Kaplan; Jackie Killeen; Julie Kudo; Nadine McMains; Craig Mohr; Marolyn Peterson; Patti Piatt; Michael Roberts, Trumps; Mitsuyo Tanaka; Jane Waddington; and Susan Williams.

Recipe Credits

Brian Ackerman, executive chef, Michael's of Monterey Bay, Watsonville: Duck Liver and Forest Mushroom Pâté
Patsy Allen, Crème de la Crème Catering, Los Angeles: Coconut-Raspberry Madeleines
Eleanor Innes: Grannie's Shortbread
Michael Roberts, chef/partner, Trumps, Los Angeles: Trumps Dill Bread
Hollie Stotter, Hollie's Moveable Feast, Los Angeles: Stilton Cheesecake
Carolyn Thacker, Gourmet Foods Instructor, Santa Monica College: Apricot Mist Punch, Mushroom Tarts
Sharon Winn, White Swan and Petite Auberge bed-and-breakfast inns, San Francisco: Artichoke Dip

Front cover Chocolate-Raspberry Truffle Cheesecake makes a delectable accompaniment to a hearty cup of tea. The recipe is on page 84.

Copyright © 1988 Chevron Chemical Company

All rights reserved under international and Pan-American copyright conventions.
No part of this book may be reproduced in any form without the written permission of 101 Productions.
Printed and bound in the U.S.A.
Published by 101 Productions and distributed by Ortho Information Services, Box 5047, San Ramon, CA 94583.

Library of Congress Catalog Card Number 88-72352
ISBN 0-89721-182-0

Publisher
Robert J. Dolezal

Editorial Director
Christine Robertson

Production Director
Ernie S. Tasaki

Managing Editor, Cookbooks
Sally W. Smith

System Manager
Katherine L. Parker

Contributors

Illustrator
Edith Allgood

Copy Chief
Melinda E. Levine

Editorial Coordinator
Cass Dempsey

Copyeditor
Lorna Cunkle

Proofreader
Karen K. Johnson

Indexer
Elinor Lindheimer

Editorial Assistant
Tamara Mallory

Layout and pagination by
Linda M. Bouchard

Series format design by
Craig Bergquist

Production by
Studio 165

Separations and printing by
W.A. Krueger Company

Contents

Introduction, *5*
Teatime in England, *9*
All About Tea, *12*
Tea Accoutrements, *16*
Tea Sandwiches, *18*

MENUS

The Elevenses, *24*
Autumn High Tea, *29*
Winter Cream Tea, *35*
Valentine's Day Tea, *40*
Bridal Shower, *48*
A May Day Picnic, *56*
High Tea With Asian Flavors, *61*
Afternoon Wedding Reception, *67*
Southwestern Jalapeño High Tea, *75*
Grazing on Melrose, *80*
Nibbling Around Nob Hill, *85*
A Very British Farm Tea, *92*
A Collector's High Tea, *97*
Tea at Three, *103*
Teddy Bear Tea, *112*
High Tea Before the Theater, *118*
Tea Dansant Buffet, *123*
Holiday Dessert Tea, *131*

•

Where to Enjoy Afternoon Tea, *139*
U.S. Measure and Metric Measure Conversion Chart, *140*
Index, *141*

Introduction

This past Christmas, I invited a few close friends to my home for an informal afternoon tea. We all agreed it was the perfect time of day to relax over delicious food and pleasant conversation, especially during the hectic holiday season. That day my tea cart was bedecked with a beautiful linen cloth, lace-trimmed napkins, and a silver tea service. An array of dainty sandwiches, tarts, and cookies, plus a decanter of sherry, were the refreshments. The event was a huge success and will probably become an annual affair.

If you've ever had the good fortune to travel in England or to entertain a visitor from the British Isles in your home, you most probably know that for the English, tea is both a beverage and a meal. The pause for tea and tea fare represents an opportunity to relax in a most civilized manner with congenial companions, or, if you are alone, a delightful chance to enjoy the solitary pleasure of reading the day's correspondence or a chapter of this week's best-seller. Teatime is a pleasant and purposeful retreat from the pressures of the outside world.

The United States is seeing a renaissance of interest in this very English institution. Over the past several years, food magazines and newspaper food sections have featured numerous articles on every aspect of tea preparation and tea equipment, plus recipes for traditional tea foods. Throughout the United States, restaurants and hotels—both grand and small—have added tea menus or expanded upon already existing ones. Americans are realizing what their English cousins have known for several hundred years—that the ceremony, ritual, and tradition of this specialized meal form a pleasant antidote to an increasingly frantic pace of life. Even if only once in a while, we are making an effort to incorporate time for tea into our busy schedules.

The First Tea

The brief respite known as afternoon tea is said to have been the creation of Anna, seventh duchess of Bedford, in the nineteenth century. At that time dinner was served fashionably late in the evening. The English upper classes ate a hearty breakfast, paused for a light lunch, and then didn't return to the table at all during the rest of the day. Understandably hungry, the duchess asked to have a small meal served in her private quarters in the late afternoon. Eventually, she thought to invite close friends to share the repast. The sensible custom was quickly adopted throughout England. Then, as now, afternoon tea was a mini-meal consisting of small sandwiches, breads, and sweets, plus a pot of hot tea.

The break for tea soon became part of daily life at all levels of English society. For the agricultural and working classes, *high tea* represented the evening meal. Served at the end of the work day, it was a hearty spread of savory pies, leftover roasted meats, and cakes. Children of the well-to-do ate in their rooms with their nannies. Menus for these nursery teas offered comforting puddings and custards, soft sandwiches, and sweet cakes. The English also devised an equivalent of our morning coffee break, called the elevenses.

Tea in the Modern Manner

As I become more involved with tea, as both a teacher and a host, I have come to realize that much confusion exists in America about this English custom. To many of my students and friends, tea is a charming holdover from the Victorian era, proper only in the late afternoon with tea fare always consisting of crustless sandwiches, petits fours, and other finger foods, served on tiered china stands.

Although a traditional tea, such as my Christmas party, does include many dishes served in the time-honored Victorian fashion, teatime can also be more substantial and afford the host a wonderful opportunity to compose menus blending familiar, well-loved tea dishes with the best of contemporary foods. And its sampler format of small bites of many foods suits the current preference for lighter preparations and smaller portions, a trend restaurant reviewers and food writers have dubbed *grazing*.

As interpreted by some of the most creative young chefs in the United States, tea menus often incorporate nontraditional ingredients presented in unexpected ways. With the introduction of afternoon tea in the Los Angeles area at Trumps, my colleagues and I—the food writers and cooking teachers of southern California—have had an exciting place to meet and experience what I call "teatime, California style."

Especially at some of the more innovative restaurants like Trumps, teatime might include fresh Santa Barbara shrimp or a lightly tossed salad topped with grilled fish or poultry and strewn with colorful edible flowers. Sandwiches and tarts are garnished with just-picked locally grown specialty produce such as daikon sprouts, *enoki* mushrooms, red bell peppers, kiwifruit, strawberries, or raspberries. Salads are lightly dressed and sauces added with restraint, just enough to tease the palate. Menus are an eclectic, international mix that reflects an increased interest in ethnic and regional foods. European and Middle Eastern pastries share billing with Asian sushi and dim sum, French pâtés, and Maryland crab cakes.

Teatime Menus

Whether in its native England or as interpreted in the "colonies," teatime can be a simple pause during the day or a multicourse meal. It can be casual or formal, for two persons or two hundred. It might include many elaborate dishes or just a cup of tea and a few sweets. The food can be as familiar as sandwiches and scones or as avant-garde as vegetable fritters and jalapeño-sparked blue cornmeal muffins. The tea meal can be as flexible and reflective of mood as you wish.

The menus I have created for this book feature a core of well-loved traditional tea foods, such as savory pies and tarts, plus an exciting array of creative contemporary dishes. All reflect what is fresh and in season. Some of the recipes have a decided southwestern heat, not surprising from a California author addicted to hot flavors.

You will find menus for every occasion and for every time of day. Included are celebrations for afternoon tea, high tea, a bridal shower, a wedding reception, a tea dance, and even a teddy bear tea for children that adults will also love. With the help of this book, you can organize a brunch, a southwestern supper, a picnic, or a pre-theater gala. If you'd like to splurge with a formal afternoon tea for a large group, you'll find helpful suggestions for planning and preparation.

With a cup of freshly brewed tea, please join me as you browse through *Teatime Celebrations*. It doesn't matter whether you pour from a polished silver tea service or a simple pottery teapot, or whether you sip from a delicate china cup or a homey earthenware mug, the result is the same: body and spirit are recharged and refreshed.

Patricia Gentry

Photograph, page 10: An inviting table—beautifully set with fine china, embroidered linens, a silver tea service, and fresh flowers—creates an elegant mood for afternoon tea. Dainty sandwiches and bite-sized pastries are classic tea fare.

Teatime in England

The English enjoy tea and tea foods throughout the day, casually or more formally, according to established custom and ritual. The serving of tea can mark a celebration or note the change of season. Some of the menus in this book are for special occasions, while others are less traditional and a bit more whimsical and personal. The following are some of the best-known English teatime meals.

Afternoon Tea

Traditionally, afternoon tea appears at 4:00 to 4:30 p.m., but any time between 3:00 and 5:00 p.m. is acceptable. It is sometimes referred to as low tea. The usual fare for afternoon tea is tea sandwiches, thinly sliced bread with butter and preserves, scones with jam, and an assortment of dainty pastries, tarts, and cookies. The menu may be expanded or varied, depending on the type of tea being served. The drawing room or library is the most common setting. The host brews the tea at the table and pours for guests. Conversation is light and noncontroversial.

Formal afternoon tea is an elaborate affair for a large group of people. Both food and beverages are set out on a buffet table. Usually, tea is poured at one end and coffee at the other. Finger foods that can be eaten standing are the rule, as most often there isn't enough seating for every guest. See Planning a Formal Afternoon Tea, pages 14 and 15.

When only a few guests are served, the meal is known as an informal tea, even though fine linens, silver, and bone china may be very much in evidence. With a small group, it is possible to offer foods that can be eaten with a fork off a small plate, such as a light salad, savory tart, charlotte, cake, or steamed pudding.

Cream Tea

When thick, clotted cream, such as Devonshire cream, is the spread offered for scones rather than the more usual butter, the tea is transformed into a cream tea. According to etiquette, preserves are spooned on the bread first, before the cream. Whipped cream can substitute for Devonshire cream.

Elevenses

Not surprisingly, this midmorning break was so dubbed because it usually occurs at 11:00 a.m. Its purpose is the same as an American morning coffee break—a moment to catch one's breath, refresh, and renew before getting on with the business of the day. With little formality about it, this simple repast consists of tea and scones or a pastry.

Ham Tea

Ham appears frequently on British tea menus. In Scotland, a post-funeral ham tea is a long-standing custom. It is a substantial meal featuring sliced ham and various breads for making sandwiches.

High Tea

A hearty affair, high tea is the evening meal, usually served at 6:00 p.m. A supper with tea, it originated with the farm and working people of the British Isles and is still popular in parts of England and Scotland, especially among the working class. The foods are filling and include savory meat puddings and pies, tasty breads with butter and jam, and assorted cakes. High tea is served at the table in the dining room or eating area.

Nursery Tea

When supper is eaten away from the grown-ups' domain—the dining room—in the privacy of the children's own quarters, it is called a nursery tea. Nanny is in charge (if the family has one). The food is soft, soothing, and often sweet. Puddings, little sandwiches, sweet biscuits, and cakes are the rule—dishes for which the English never seem to outgrow their childhood fondness.

Strawberry Tea

In late spring the first-of-the-season strawberries are the inspiration and focal point of a strawberry tea. The berries are served as a separate course, accompanied by clotted cream. Strawberries and cream have always been part of the teas served at summer sporting events, a custom most notably followed today at the famous tennis matches held each June at Wimbledon.

Summer Tea

On warm sunny days tea moves out to the garden or lawn. The fruits of summer are celebrated, especially strawberries and raspberries. Sweet, juicy peaches, nectarines, and apricots are also popular choices.

Winter Tea

With a menu that includes toast, crumpets, and tea breads, a winter tea might be cozily enjoyed on trays or individual tables in front of a merrily blazing fire. In the past, toast was browned over the coals in the fireplace, held at a safe distance on the end of a long-handled implement called a toasting fork.

All About Tea

The taste of a tea depends on where it is grown, the climate, the type of tea (black, oolong, or green), and whether it has been scented or flavored. Herbal teas are not included here since they are not technically true teas but blends of ingredients such as spices, herbs, and fruit peels. Some tea drinkers prefer herbal teas because they contain no caffeine and they offer a choice of interesting flavors.

Tea, *Camellia sinensis*, is an evergreen plant grown generally in tropical and semitropical climates. It will grow from sea level to 10,000 feet, and in areas with rainfall as low as 50 inches or as high as 300 inches. It grows best in well-drained acid soil, in a warm, tropical climate. However, most of the finest flavored teas grow at a cooler, higher altitude. The most noteworthy tea-producing countries are India, Sri Lanka, China, Taiwan, Japan, and Indonesia. Tea is also grown in the Soviet Union, Iran, Turkey, and certain areas of Africa and South America, but these teas are not considered particularly outstanding.

Tea leaves are harvested at various times during the year, but the first and second flushings usually produce the highest and most sought-after quality. A flushing is a set of new leaves, specifically two leaves and a bud for average-to-good tea and only the growth bud and the next youngest leaf for a premium-quality tea. Prime teas are made only from first flush tea leaves. So expensive and desirable is the first flush of certain teas (Darjeeling, for example) that most of it is bought at auction by private tea connoisseurs and select European tea merchants.

Other factors that affect the quality and price of tea are the yearly climate and growing conditions, the elevation where the tea is grown, the processing at the plantation, and even the political situation of the country.

Forms of Tea

Loose Tea Leaves This form is preferred by purists. The leaves have plenty of room for expansion, and thus release a full flavor. One pound loose tea, using 1 teaspoon per cup of water, will yield about 200 cups of tea.

Tea Bags Each bag is a premeasured spoonful of tea leaves in special filter paper. Tea bags can yield a good cup of tea if the tea leaves are of high quality. Buy reputable brands.

Instant Tea This water-soluble powder is most often used for quick iced tea. Those who really enjoy tea prefer to make iced tea from the same high-quality tea they drink hot.

Tea Processing

Tea is processed to preserve the leaves and concentrate their flavor. Processing involves one or more of four basic operations: *withering*, which removes as much moisture as possible from the leaves; *rolling*, which breaks up the cell structure of the dried leaves to release natural juices and fragrances; *fermentation*, which exposes the leaves to air (oxygen changes the color of the leaves from green to copper or black); and *firing* or *drying*, which stops the oxidation process and dries the leaves evenly.

Depending upon processing, tea is classified as one of three types: fermented or black; semifermented or oolong; and unfermented or green.

Fermented or black tea Black tea, which is subjected to all four processing operations, accounts for approximately 97 percent of the tea consumed in the United States. The flavor of tea brewed from black tea leaves is rich and strong.

Semifermented or oolong tea Oolong tea is lightly withered, rolled, and only partially fermented prior to being dried. The leaves are half copper and half black. The flavor of oolong tea is rich and fruity and not as strong as that of black tea.

Unfermented or green tea Green tea is not fermented. The leaves, which are steamed or heated, then rolled and dried, are green because they have not been oxidized. When brewed, green tea is light and clear with a delicate, fresh flavor. Of the three types, green tea has the least amount of caffeine.

What's in a Name?

Orange pekoe (pronounced PEE-ko), *flowery orange pekoe, pekoe, broken orange pekoe, fannings,* and *dust* are terms used to denote leaf size only. Orange pekoe and flowery orange pekoe refer to very long or very large tea leaves. One of the best ways to see the difference in tea leaf size is to purchase a small amount of silver tip oolong tea and compare the leaves with those you find in a tea bag. Most tea bags contain a large percent of fannings, perhaps some dust, and only a few large tea leaves. Fannings and dust are used in tea bags because they brew more quickly and because it is more difficult to pack large leaves in tea bags and keep the size uniform. They are also used in the production of instant tea. Fannings and dust are not necessarily of poor quality; quality is determined more by type of tea. However, it is generally conceded that a clearer, more full-bodied cup of tea is brewed with a loose, expensive tea, generally an orange pekoe or a flowery orange pekoe.

The name of a tea can come from the name of a specific growing area or it can be a proprietary name formulated for a certain tea blend. Tea merchants have historically blended tea for valued clients such as Lady Londonderry (noted for her salons during the early 1900s), Earl Grey, and J. P. Morgan, and for certain clubs and hotels, which sometimes then made these teas available to the general public. Teas are also blended for a specific clientele; examples are Dowager, Nursery, or Invalid tea.

A Tea Sampler

Developing a palate for tea is much like developing one for wine. It takes tasting, remembering (perhaps noting reactions on cards), education, and experimentation. Pairing teas with appropriate foods is important. Teas can be smoky, earthy, flowery, malty, nutty, fruity, or spicy. To match a smoky tea with southwestern food would be logical; to serve the same smoky tea with dainty afternoon tea sandwiches and pastries would be inappropriate.

The following list of teas and tea blends includes those that are readily available and popular.

Assam A bold tea from India with malted hints, Assam brews a deep color and is excellent for high tea and for drinking during the winter months. Golden tip Assam is particularly full-bodied and pleasant.

Ceylon Grown at high altitudes, this premium-quality tea brews a bright cup of tea that turns a golden color when milk is added.

China Rose This black tea scented with rose petals is a light, refreshing brew. It is an interesting tea to serve with the light fare of afternoon tea, with a light dessert, or at the conclusion of a special-occasion tea luncheon.

Darjeeling The premium qualities of Darjeeling make it one of the most expensive teas in the world. The underlying flavors are flowery or reminiscent of black currants and muscat grape. Often called the champagne of teas, Darjeeling is most appropriate for afternoon tea and for special occasions.

Decaffeinated Caffeine is chemically leached out and the tea is redried. For those tea drinkers who cannot have caffeine, these teas offer the opportunity to experience some of the specialty teas.

Earl Grey This delightful tea is scented with oil of bergamot (bergamot is a Mediterranean citrus fruit often used in perfume making). Earl Grey is frequently served at afternoon tea in the United States. Along with English Breakfast, it is the leading imported specialty tea.

English and Irish Breakfast Both these teas are usually a blend of good-quality Indian and Ceylon teas. The Irish is the stronger tea of the two. The blends vary from company to company; some include a small amount of Keemun. Tasting and comparing brands will help you determine which you prefer.

Formosa Oolong This deliciously fruity tea from China has little bitterness or astringency and goes well with light foods and desserts—a perfect choice for afternoon tea. It is considered among the finest of teas.

Fruit-flavored There are many flavored teas, such as black currant, apricot, lemon, lime, orange, and peach. The flavoring is sprayed onto black tea leaves. These teas are pleasant served for afternoon tea or to accompany desserts, especially fruit desserts; they also make delicious iced tea.

Gunpowder The leaves of this special green tea from China are rolled into tiny, compact pellets, which is why the tea got its name. Gunpowder brews thin, pale, slightly bitter-tasting tea that is light yellowish green in color. It is a favorite in Asia.

Jasmine This is a beautifully scented, large-leaf, semifermented tea that usually contains some dried jasmine flowers. It is a lovely tea to have with certain Asian foods, especially dim sum.

Keemun The most famous of the China black teas, this low-grown tea is sweet, fruity, and full-bodied. Keemun is the one tea that gains additional character from aging; a Keemun that has aged for a year is often described as a Winey Keemun. Keemun was the tea of Imperial China.

Lapsang Souchong A large-leaf tea from China with a strong taste of wood smoke and tar, this tea gained fame due to its appearances in the works of Agatha Christie. Lapsang souchong should be drunk for its bracing qualities. It is also a good match for smoked food and earthy cuisines.

Planning a Formal Afternoon Tea

Careful planning will ensure a successfully staged tea affair. Here are some suggestions to make the preparation move smoothly and to give you the time to actually enjoy your tea.

Menu *For a tea reception where all guests will not be seated, serve only finger foods that are easily eaten in one or two bites. The menu should include small tea sandwiches, tea breads with fillings that are not drippy, filled vegetable bases (such as endive leaves and cherry tomatoes), bite-sized cookies, and tarts.*

Incorporate some foods in the menu that can be made well ahead and frozen or prepared two or three days in advance and refrigerated. Pastry shells and cakes can be made ahead and frozen. Fruit curd fillings keep well.

Pâtés and spreads can be made at least a day or two in advance. The base for the punch can be made the day before. Sandwich fillings can be made the day before, but the sandwiches should be assembled the day of the affair. They will keep for several hours if covered with both a damp cloth and plastic wrap.

Linens, China, Silver, Flowers, Music *At least 2 weeks in advance of your afternoon tea, check on the condition of any stored items. Have linens cleaned and pressed, china washed and ready, and silver polished. Plan centerpieces and order any flowers you need. If entertainment is planned—such as a pianist or harpist— you may need to select and engage a performer 4 to 6 months in advance.*

Lung Ching Another China tea, this tea is also called Dragon Well (named for a spring that runs near Hangzhou, a city in eastern China that was at one time the country's capital). It brews a light emerald tea with a grassy flavor. It is low in caffeine.

Pingsuey Translated from the Chinese, *pingsuey* means *ice water*. It is a mild and delicately flavored black tea.

Russian-Style Up until the very early part of the twentieth century, tea traveled to Russia from China on the backs of camels and was known as Russian Caravan tea. The caravans have disappeared, but the designations *Russian* and *Russian Caravan* remain (perhaps because of their romantic associations) on a diverse assortment of tea blends. These blends have only their name in common, since they vary from company to company.

Silver Tip Oolong A very long-leafed Chinese tea with a full rich flavor, this brews a tea that is slightly fruity, with no bitterness and little astringency.

Yunnan Brewing a rich, coppery infusion, Yunnan is grown in China at elevations from 3,000 to 7,000 feet, with that grown highest being the best quality. It has a rich, full-bodied, slightly nutty taste.

The Perfect Cup of Tea

The goal when preparing a cup of tea is to brew just the length of time needed, but not so long that the tannins, which make the tea bitter, will be released. Brewing time usually ranges from 3 to 5 minutes, but may go up to 6 minutes for some of the very long-leaf types, especially if the leaves are tightly rolled. The English enjoy milk with their tea, never cream, which is thought to make the tea cloudy. Milk, always cold and very fresh, is usually added first, then the hot tea (milk and tea are thought by many to mix better if the milk precedes the tea, but this is an arguable point among tea fanciers). Sweeteners and lemon are optional.

1. Bring freshly drawn, cold water to a full, rolling boil. In hard water areas, use bottled or filtered water. Plan to brew the tea as soon as the water reaches the boiling point. Water that is boiled for an extended period of time loses oxygen, which affects the taste of the tea.

2. Rinse a ceramic pot with very hot water to preheat it. A pot made of aluminum or other metal that will impart an off-taste to the tea is not recommended.

3. Measure tea into heated pot. A long-standing rule is 1 teaspoon per cup, plus 1 teaspoon for the pot. Sometimes a little more of the long-leaf teas, such as oolong, is needed. Loose tea generally gives the richest flavor.

4. Pour boiling water into pot; if using loose tea, stir.

5. Place lid on pot and brew 3 to 5 minutes. The color of the tea varies depending on the type of tea used. Some teas brew light and others are very dark. Correct time, rather than color, should be the guide. If you prefer a weak tea, brew full strength and then dilute with boiling water.

6. To serve, remove tea bags or strain tea into cups or into a special serving teapot (silver, bone china, or any attractive pot made of a nonreactive material).

7. If you wish to use a tea cozy, wait until after the tea has been brewed and strained, and the first few cups have been served. (You want to avoid "stewing" the tea while it is brewing.) Cover the pot to keep the remaining tea warm.

Tea Accoutrements

Teapots appear in many shapes and with all sorts of decoration. Throughout history, teapots and other tea ware were often embellished with designs that commemorated historical events; these are very popular with collectors. There are also whimsical teapots intended for the nursery set and teapots with a contemporary feeling, often with matching cups. In addition to pots for brewing and serving tea and cups for drinking, hundreds of specialty accoutrements have been developed related to tea. By the end of the last century, some silver manufacturers offered as many as 250 individual pieces within one pattern. If you do a little sleuthing in antique shops, you may come across sugar tongs, lemon forks, lettuce servers, sandwich servers, asparagus forks and servers, strawberry forks, runcible spoons, compote servers, butter picks, grape scissors, sauce ladles, lobster scissors and picks, mustard spoons, and more. They really are lovely pieces, many with dainty filigree work and hand-chased ornamentation. The most common tea ware includes the following.

Caddy Spoon

Because a caddy spoon has a very short handle it can easily be mistaken for a child's spoon—except the bowl is unusually large. A caddy spoon is used to scoop tea leaves from the caddy (see Tea Caddy). Many are made of silver.

Lemon Fork

How else to serve the ubiquitous thin slices of lemon that appear on every tea table but with a special lemon fork? Lemon forks usually have distinctive, very curved outer tines that flare away from the handle.

Mote Spoon

The filigree openings or mesh in a mote spoon are designed for straining stray tea leaves from the poured tea. (A mote is a particle.) This spoon also has a sharp point to clean the spout of the teapot should it become clogged.

Infuser

Also known as a tea ball, an infuser is a perforated hollow container that holds the tea during brewing. The perforations allow the hot water to reach the tea without the leaves spreading throughout the liquid. It is removed when the brew is of the desired strength.

Strainer

When tea is brewed with loose leaves, a strainer is placed over a teacup and the tea is poured through; the strainer traps the leaves and allows the liquid to flow into the cup. Many beautiful antique strainers were crafted by silversmiths. Some are a combination of gold and silver or enamel and silver.

Tea Caddy

A caddy is a small box, can, or chest for storing loose tea. Its name derives from *catty*, a Malay word meaning a unit of weight of around $1\frac{1}{3}$ pounds. Antique tea caddies can be very ornate, often fashioned of silver, brass, copper, pewter, or china. Many are equipped with a lock because tea was a valuable commodity.

Tea Cozy

This fabric cover, put over the teapot, helps keep tea warm—or cozy. The tea cozy may be made from quilted fabrics and embroidered with stitchery, or done in tapestry, knit, or crocheted. Victorian needlepoint cozies were sometimes richly beaded.

Tea Accoutrements

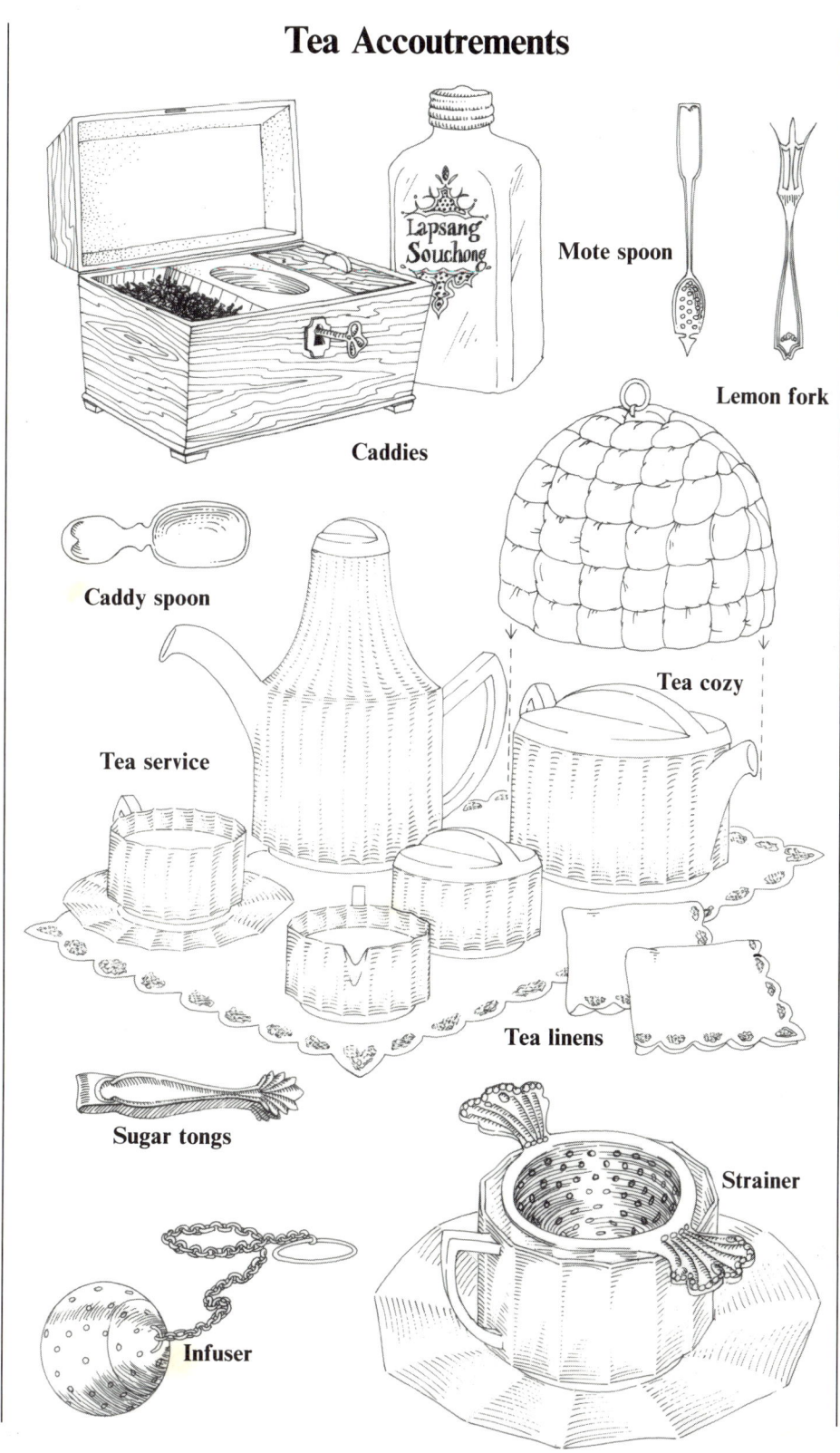

Teatime Celebrations

Tea Linens

Small, square, delicate linen tablecloths and napkins are customary for the tea table. Often embroidered, they can be quite beautiful. Unfortunately, tablecloths of the proper size and shape are rarely sold new anymore. You may have better luck at antique shops that sell vintage clothing and linens, at rummage sales, or at swap meets. If you have a talent for sewing and embroidery, consider making your own.

Tea Service

Silver or bone china sets, the focal point of a lovely afternoon tea, set the proper mood. The tea service should include teapot, sugar bowl, tongs, and pitcher for milk (not cream). It may also include a waste receptacle for any tea leaves that wind up in the teacup. Some sets come with a large pot designed to hold hot water for brewing and for diluting strong tea. If using a pot made of a metal other than silver, be sure that it is nonreactive so that the tea doesn't develop an off-taste or -color.

Tea Sandwiches

Tea sandwiches are meant to be tasty tidbits, enticements rather than filling fare. Crusts are trimmed away for the most delicate types. Breads for sandwiches need to be firm and even in texture. A variety of thinly sliced breads—white, whole wheat, raisin-nut, and herb—offer a contrast of textures and tastes. For ribbon sandwiches and sandwich loaves (see pages 22 and 23), purchase unsliced bread at the bakery. Breads for more substantial meals like a high tea might be dense and chewy; pumpernickel, black bread, and onion bread are a few suggestions.

Creative Sandwich Ideas

A myriad of possible combinations for tea sandwiches are created by mixing breads, rolls, fillings, spreads, flavored butters, and garnishes. Following are some conventional as well as some unusual sandwich ideas. When using mayonnaise-based fillings, moist fruits, or vegetable slices, lightly butter the bread first. The butter will prevent the bread from getting soggy. Since many of the fillings are already seasoned, use unsalted butter to keep a balance of flavor.

Hearty Sandwiches

Served with a tasty bowl of soup, a hearty sandwich is a satisfying main course for a high tea menu. Start with a selection of breads, sandwich rolls, croissants, or pita bread, and then fill them with equally substantial ingredients.
- Croissant stuffed with Tearoom Chicken Salad (see page 53)
- Grilled chicken with Jalapeño Jelly (see page 79) glaze on grilled French bread
- Grilled sun-dried tomato, blue cheese, and mozzarella cheese on sourdough bread
- Lox, whipped cream cheese, thinly sliced tomatoes on sliced miniature bagels
- Sliced pork with Cranberry Chutney (see page 95) on homemade biscuits
- Smoked ham and Emmenthaler cheese on dark bread, served with Dijon-style mustard and peach or mango chutney
- Thinly sliced roast beef, sprigs of arugula or watercress, and Fresh Tomato-Mint Chutney (see page 83) on onion rolls

---

An Informal Spread of Fruit and Cheese

A glass of port accompanied by a selection of cheese, fruit, and imported water biscuits makes a nice informal afternoon tea break. The following are some cheeses and fruits well-suited for this presentation.

Cheese *Asiago, Brie, Brillat-Savarin, Camembert, Edam, Gorgonzola, Gouda, sharp New York or Canadian Cheddar, smoked Gouda, Stilton.*

Fruit *Bosc and Comice pears, fresh figs, fresh raspberries, Gala apples, Lady apples.*

Open-Faced Sandwiches

Keep these sandwiches simple, but always aim for a contrast of colors and textures. If possible, cut them into decorative shapes with a cookie cutter.

- Basil-Parmesan Mayonnaise (see below) and thinly sliced tomatoes or sliced chicken or turkey on whole wheat bread
- Chutney Cream Cheese (see below) and sliced fruit or edible flowers on raisin bread
- Peanut Butter Filling (see page 20), sliced bananas, and shredded coconut on cinnamon bread
- Pecan Butter (see page 21) and sliced smoked chicken on whole-grain bread
- Raspberry Butter (see page 21) and sliced strawberries or nectarines, or a combination, on white bread
- Smoked Salmon Spread (see page 41), golden caviar, and daikon radish sprout garnish on dill bread
- Tomato Butter (see page 21), fresh basil leaves, tomato slices, and baby shrimp on herb bread
- Watercress Mayonnaise (see page 21), cucumber slice, and watercress leaf or radish slice garnish on white bread

Tea Sandwich Fillings

Fish pastes, meat salads, flavored butters and mayonnaises, cucumber slices, sprigs of fresh greens—these are the familiar sandwich fillings of the tea table, but don't limit yourself to what's been done before, or to only savory combinations. Fruit- or nut-flavored spreads are refreshing and can reflect the seasons.

Avocado-Bacon Spread

- 6 slices bacon, cooked and crumbled
- 2 ripe avocados, peeled and mashed
- 2 tablespoons finely chopped onion
- 2 tablespoons fresh lemon juice
- 3 tablespoons mayonnaise
- Salt and freshly ground pepper, to taste
- 1 tablespoon minced cilantro (optional)
- 1 tablespoon finely minced jalapeño chile (optional)

Combine bacon, avocados, onion, lemon juice, and mayonnaise. Taste and season with salt and pepper. Mix in cilantro and jalapeño, if desired.

Makes 1½ cups

Basil-Parmesan Mayonnaise

- 1 cup mayonnaise
- ⅓ cup minced basil leaves
- 3 tablespoons freshly grated Parmesan cheese

Combine all ingredients.

Makes 1¼ cups

Chutney Cream Cheese

- 8 ounces cream cheese, softened
- ¼ teaspoon ground cinnamon or cardamom
- ½ cup prepared chutney or Cranberry Chutney (see page 95) finely chopped

Combine all ingredients.

Makes 1½ cups

Dill-Mint Mayonnaise

1 cup mayonnaise
⅓ cup snipped dill
1 to 2 tablespoons minced fresh mint

Combine all ingredients.

Makes 1¼ cups

Egg-Olive Filling

4 hard-cooked eggs, peeled and chopped
2 tablespoons minced green onion
¼ cup mayonnaise
¼ cup chopped pimiento-stuffed green olives
Salt and freshly ground pepper, to taste

Combine all ingredients.

Makes approximately 1½ cups

Ham Salad Filling

2 cups minced cooked ham
⅔ cup minced sweet pickle
2 tablespoons finely minced onion
¼ teaspoon hot-pepper sauce
½ cup mayonnaise
1 tablespoon Dijon-style mustard

Combine all ingredients.

Makes 3 cups

Herb Butter

½ cup unsalted butter, softened
1½ teaspoons fresh lemon juice
2 to 3 tablespoons minced fresh herbs or combination of herbs (see Note)

In bowl of food processor, combine ingredients; blend until smooth. Refrigerate in covered container. Bring to room temperature before using.

Makes ½ cup

Note Suggested herb mixtures include: 2 tablespoons minced oregano and 1 tablespoon minced basil; 2 tablespoons minced tarragon and 1 teaspoon finely grated lemon rind; 2 tablespoons minced fresh dill and 1 tablespoon minced chives; 2 tablespoons minced chervil and 1 teaspoon finely grated orange rind.

Peanut Butter Filling

1 cup chunky peanut butter
2 tablespoons honey
3 tablespoons finely chopped raisins

Combine all ingredients.

Makes about 1¼ cups

Pecan Butter

½ cup unsalted butter, softened
¼ cup finely chopped toasted pecans
1 teaspoon brown sugar
Pinch freshly grated nutmeg
1 teaspoon fresh lemon juice

In bowl of food processor, combine ingredients; blend until smooth. Refrigerate in covered container. Bring to room temperature before using.

Makes ½ cup

Raspberry Butter

½ cup unsalted butter, softened
2 teaspoons fresh lemon juice
4 tablespoons seedless raspberry jam

In bowl of food processor, combine ingredients; blend until smooth. Refrigerate in covered container. Bring to room temperature before using.

Makes ½ cup

Shrimp Filling

8 ounces cooked bay shrimp
⅓ cup minced celery
⅓ cup finely chopped water chestnuts or blanched almonds
¼ teaspoon salt
2 teaspoons snipped dill
6 tablespoons mayonnaise

Combine all ingredients.

Makes 2 cups

Tomato Butter

½ cup unsalted butter, softened
1 tablespoon tomato paste
1 teaspoon fresh lemon juice
1 teaspoon finely minced fresh rosemary
⅛ teaspoon white pepper

In bowl of food processor combine ingredients; blend until smooth. Refrigerate in covered container. Bring to room temperature before using.

Makes ½ cup

Watercress Mayonnaise

½ cup mayonnaise
¼ cup minced watercress
⅛ teaspoon celery salt
⅛ teaspoon white pepper

Combine all ingredients.

Makes about ¾ cup

Special Presentations

Bread and filling can combine in many unexpected and visually attractive ways. Stacked layers can make stripes or be rolled into pinwheels. A hollowed loaf of bread can become an edible container for tea sandwiches. Consider trying the following.

Bread Basket

Select dense bread that has a close-grained texture and a strong crust. Larger loaves (at least 2½ pounds) work best. Trim 1 inch from the top of the loaf. Cut all around the inside edges to leave a ½-inch wall of crust. To remove the interior of the loaf in one piece, cut into the side of the loaf ⅜ inch from the bottom of the crust. Rotate point of knife back and forth to free bread from bottom. To completely detach the bread, repeat with three more incisions, spaced evenly around the loaf. Lift out the bread. Partially freeze the cut-out bread; trim to an even shape. Cut bread into thin, even slices. Assemble sandwiches with desired fillings. When sandwiches are completed, dip edges in chopped parsley. For added appeal, line the bread basket with curly lettuce. Arrange sandwiches inside and garnish with sprigs of fresh parsley or dill, radish roses and green onion fans, or colorful edible flowers.

Pinwheel Sandwiches

Remove crust from unsliced, very fresh bread. Cut lengthwise in slices as thin as possible. Lightly flatten bread with rolling pin. Spread evenly with softened butter and any well-seasoned, minced sandwich filling. Roll each slice tightly and wrap in aluminum foil or plastic wrap. Chill, seam-side down, until firm. When ready to serve, cut in thin slices crosswise.

Pita Swirls

With a serrated bread knife, split 6-inch pita bread rounds in half horizontally. Stack the halves between layers of dampened paper towels and cover with plastic wrap. Let bread sit at room temperature for about an hour to soften. Working with one pita half at a time, spread a filling on rough side of each half. Roll up pita tightly, jelly-roll style, and wrap tightly with plastic wrap. Chill rolls for several hours. To serve, cut rolls crosswise into ¼-inch-thick slices.

Ribbon Sandwiches

Made of contrasting layers of bread and filling, ribbon sandwiches have many creative possibilities. Vary the kind of bread used: white, wheat, dill, raisin. Select at least two different kinds of bread to alternate with the fillings. Remove crusts and cut unsliced loaves lengthwise in ½-inch slices. Choose spreads and fillings that complement each other. Spread softened butter on one side of each slice of bread, then spread fillings on each lengthwise slice except for top slice. Stack slices, placing top slice buttered side down. Cut crosswise in ½-inch slices to expose the striped pattern; to serve, cut each slice in thirds.

Sandwich Loaf

A sandwich loaf is created in the same way as are ribbon sandwiches. It differs in that it is frosted and the loaf is presented whole. Trim away all crust and cut horizontally down the length of the loaf in four or five slices. Spread a filling on each slice of bread except for top slice, using a different filling for each layer; stack slices. When complete, spread loaf with a cream cheese frosting (12 ounces cream cheese mixed with 2 tablespoons whipping cream). Garnish frosted loaf with sliced vegetables, fresh herbs, or edible flowers, if desired, arranged in an attractive pattern.

Special Presentations

Bread basket

Ribbon sandwiches

Pita swirls

Sandwich loaf

Pinwheel sandwiches

Teatime Celebrations 23

The Elevenses
Serves 6 to 8

Olallieberry Champagne Kir
Southwestern Paella
Chèvre Tart
Tropical Fruit Salad With Mango Sauce
Blueberry Whole Wheat Muffins
Orange-Glazed Oatmeal Cake
English or Irish Breakfast Tea

In England elevenses is a late-morning tea break more than a meal. I've expanded the menu into an eleven o'clock brunch. When the weather is pleasant and the meal can be served outdoors on a patio or terrace, brunch is an especially pleasant way to entertain.

This type of party does require some organization so that all is ready when the guests arrive. The paella can be prepared the day before, then baked and garnished just before serving. The Tropical Fruit Salad is best assembled the morning of the brunch so the fruits retain their texture, but the fruit can be cut up a day ahead and stored in pineapple juice in a tightly sealed container. The Mango Sauce will keep in the refrigerator for a day or so.

• OLALLIEBERRY CHAMPAGNE KIR •

The olallieberry is a cross between the youngberry and the black loganberry, a blackberry relative. The wine has a wonderful berry taste; it is also delicious served over vanilla ice cream. If desired, substitute any fruit-flavored wine.

1 cup olallieberry wine	2 bottles (750 ml each) chilled Champagne

Pour 1 to 2 tablespoons olallieberry wine into each glass. Fill with Champagne.

Serves 8

• SOUTHWESTERN PAELLA •

Millet and cumin add an inventive twist to this variation of a traditional saffron-infused Spanish rice casserole. Millet is available at health-food stores.

¼ cup dried millet	½ teaspoon salt
2 tablespoons olive oil	¾ cup diced red bell pepper (1 large pepper)
5 ounces smoked Louisiana hot sausage, cut in ¼-inch slices	2 teaspoons finely minced fresh jalapeño chile (seeds removed)
1 whole chicken breast, skinned, boned, and cut in 1-inch cubes	1 pound shrimp, shelled and deveined
1 cup chopped onion (1 large onion)	½ cup petite peas
2 cloves garlic, finely minced	½ cup corn kernels (fresh or frozen)
2 cups chicken stock	¾ cup minced cilantro, for garnish
1 cup long-grain brown or white rice	1 avocado, peeled, pitted, and sliced, for garnish
¼ cup dry white wine	Lime or lemon wedges, for accompaniment
½ teaspoon ground cumin	
⅛ teaspoon saffron	

1. To soften millet, place it in a medium saucepan, cover with warm water, and cook 8 minutes; set aside to cool in saucepan (liquid will be absorbed as millet cools).

2. In a heavy skillet or Dutch oven, heat olive oil. Add sausage and sauté until light brown (about 4 minutes). Add chicken pieces and sauté 2 minutes. Remove sausage and chicken with slotted spoon and set aside.

3. Add onion to skillet and sauté until softened (about 5 minutes); add garlic and sauté 1 minute.

4. Add millet, chicken stock, rice, wine, cumin, saffron, and salt. Bring to boil, reduce heat, cover, and cook until liquid is absorbed (25 to 30 minutes).

5. Mix in bell pepper, jalapeño chile, shrimp, peas, corn, sausage, and chicken. (Paella may be prepared ahead to this point and refrigerated.)

6. Preheat oven to 350° F; bake 20 to 25 minutes (30 to 35 minutes if paella has just been removed from refrigerator).

7. Serve warm, garnished with cilantro and avocado and accompanied with lime or lemon wedges.

Serves 8

• CHÈVRE TART •

Fresh seasonal vegetables can be substituted for the spinach, if desired. Carrots, available all year, add wonderful color. Look for chèvre at specialty cheese stores.

Single Crust Pastry (see below)
1 egg white, slightly beaten
8 ounces chèvre
¾ cup ricotta cheese
¼ cup unsalted butter, softened
3 tablespoons flour
2 egg yolks
¼ cup whipping cream
1 teaspoon minced fresh thyme

Salt and freshly ground pepper, to taste
1 bunch spinach, washed, stems removed, cooked, and thoroughly drained
5 carrots, sliced and cooked until tender
2 teaspoons minced fresh rosemary

1. Preheat oven to 400° F. Brush pastry shell with egg white. Bake shell 5 minutes; set aside to cool. Reduce heat to 375° F.

2. In a food processor purée chèvre, ricotta, butter, flour, egg yolks, cream, thyme, salt, and pepper.

3. Spoon one third of the cheese mixture into pastry shell. Chop spinach and scatter over cheese. Spoon another third of the cheese mixture on top of spinach. Scatter carrots over cheese and top with remaining cheese mixture.

4. Sprinkle rosemary over top of tart. Bake until puffy and golden brown (about 35 minutes).

Serves 6 as a main dish or 10 as an appetizer

Single Crust Pastry

1⅓ cups sifted flour
½ teaspoon salt
½ cup vegetable shortening
3 to 4 tablespoons chilled water

1. In a medium bowl combine flour and salt. With a pastry blender cut in ¼ cup vegetable shortening until mixture is crumbly. Cut in remaining ¼ cup shortening. Leave some of the pieces of shortening the size of lima beans. Add 3 tablespoons water, 1 tablespoon at a time, stirring very lightly with a fork. After 3 tablespoons have been added, gather dough into ball and press into a flat circle with smooth edges. If dough will not form a ball and seems dry, add the remaining 1 tablespoon water. Wrap in plastic and chill for 30 minutes.

2. On a lightly floured surface, roll dough into a circle about 1½ inches larger than pie plate. Carefully pick up dough and ease into pie plate (do not stretch dough). With kitchen scissors trim dough to ¾ inch beyond edge of pie plate; fold under to make a double thickness of dough around the rim and flute with fingers, fork, or pastry jagger.

3. *For a single crust baked without filling:* Prick bottom and sides thoroughly with a fork. Bake in a 425° F oven until golden brown (10 to 12 minutes). *For a single crust baked with filling:* Do not prick dough. Bake according to time and temperature recommended for filling used.

Makes one 9-inch shell

TROPICAL FRUIT SALAD WITH MANGO SAUCE

The mango is a luscious tropical fruit, with a skin that is difficult to peel. It helps to chill the mango before peeling it. A thin-bladed serrated knife works best. Slice parallel to the flat side of the large seed to remove the flesh. Slip the knife between flesh and skin and cut away skin.

- 1 pineapple, peeled and cut in wedges
- 1 papaya, peeled, seeded, and sliced
- 2 kiwifruit, peeled and sliced
- 1 cantaloupe, peeled, seeded, and sliced
- ¼ cup finely chopped candied ginger
- Mango Sauce (see below)

Arrange pineapple, papaya, kiwifruit, and cantaloupe attractively on a large serving platter. Sprinkle with chopped candied ginger. Place Mango Sauce in sauce dish and serve as an accompaniment to the tropical fruit.

Serves 6 to 8

Mango Sauce

- 1 ripe mango, peeled, pitted, and cut in chunks
- 2 tablespoons fresh lime juice
- 3 tablespoons frozen orange juice concentrate, thawed

In blender or food processor, purée mango chunks with lime juice and orange juice concentrate.

Makes about ½ cup

BLUEBERRY WHOLE WHEAT MUFFINS

Quick-cooking oatmeal may be substituted for the whole wheat cereal. Chop the oats briefly in a food processor to make a finer meal. If you prefer, bake the batter in miniature muffin tins. These muffins freeze well, wrapped airtight.

- 1 cup sifted flour
- ⅓ cup sugar
- ½ teaspoon salt
- 2½ teaspoons baking powder
- 1 cup instant whole wheat cereal
- 1 egg, beaten
- ¼ cup vegetable oil
- ¾ cup milk
- ¾ cup fresh or frozen blueberries (do not thaw if frozen)

1. Preheat oven to 400° F. Into a medium bowl sift flour, sugar, salt, and baking powder; stir in whole wheat cereal. Make a well in dry ingredients.

2. Combine egg, oil, and milk; pour into dry ingredients and stir just to combine. Do not overmix. Gently fold in blueberries.

3. Spoon batter into 12 well-greased muffin cups. Bake until lightly browned (about 20 minutes). Serve warm.

Makes 12 standard muffins or 24 to 30 miniature muffins

• ORANGE-GLAZED OATMEAL CAKE •

This oatmeal spice cake is moist and keeps very nicely. I often bring it along on camping trips. It packs well and is good to nibble at on a day hike. The glaze infuses the cake with a pleasing hint of citrus.

- 2½ cups boiling water
- 2 cups quick-cooking oatmeal
- 1 cup butter or margarine, softened
- 1 cup firmly packed brown sugar
- 2 cups granulated sugar
- 4 eggs
- 2⅔ cups sifted flour
- 1 teaspoon salt
- 2 teaspoons baking soda
- 2 teaspoons ground cinnamon
- 1½ teaspoons grated nutmeg
- 2 teaspoons vanilla extract
- Orange Glaze (see below)

1. Preheat oven to 350° F. Pour the boiling water over oatmeal and let stand.

2. In a large bowl cream together butter and sugars until mixture is light and fluffy. Beat in eggs one at a time, beating well after each addition.

3. Sift together flour, salt, baking soda, cinnamon, and nutmeg. Add flour mixture, oatmeal, and vanilla to creamed butter mixture and mix thoroughly.

4. Turn into a greased and floured 12-cup bundt pan. Bake until cake tester inserted in center comes out clean (about 70 minutes).

5. Cool cake in pan for 10 minutes. Invert cake onto wire rack. Poke holes in cake and pour glaze over top.

Serves 8

Orange Glaze

- ¼ cup granulated sugar
- 2 tablespoons water
- 2 tablespoons orange-flavored liqueur

In a medium saucepan combine granulated sugar and the water; bring to a boil over medium-high heat and stir to dissolve sugar. Remove saucepan from heat and add orange-flavored liqueur. Stir to thoroughly blend ingredients.

Makes about ¼ cup

AUTUMN HIGH TEA
Serves 6

Baked Brie With Roasted Garlic
Acorn Squash Bisque
Calico Cornmeal Scones
Roast Beef Sandwiches With Corn Relish
Southern Bourbon Cake
Beaujolais Nouveau
Assam Tea

Although a high tea is traditionally served at the dining room table, this menu is particularly nice when presented in front of a warming fire. Make the sandwiches with roast beef left over from another meal or buy the meat already cooked and sliced at a delicatessen. Beaujolais Nouveau, a fruity red French wine, is generally available after November 15. In October serve a Beaujolais-Villages.

Southern Bourbon Cake is a favorite to prepare during the busy holidays because it keeps for at least a week. It's a perfect cake to have on hand for spur-of-the-moment entertaining or to offer to unexpected guests. It also goes nicely with a glass of port, some fruit, and cheese.

Chase away autumn's chill with high tea served before a blazing fire. The menu features a rich squash bisque and hearty meat sandwiches, accompanied by garlic-topped cheese baked in a hollowed loaf of bread. The finale is a bourbon-spiked fruit cake.

• BAKED BRIE WITH ROASTED GARLIC •

To vary this impressive hors d'oeuvre, spread Jalapeño Jelly (see page 79) on top of the Brie, wrap with your own brioche dough, chill, then bake. Or, bake Brie in a hollowed loaf of French bread.

1 bulb garlic	1 small wheel Brie
1 tablespoon olive oil	1 baguette, sliced and lightly
2 tablespoons minced fresh rosemary or marjoram	toasted, for accompaniment

1. Preheat oven to 350° F. Halve garlic horizontally; brush with olive oil and sprinkle with rosemary or marjoram. Wrap garlic in aluminum foil and bake 30 minutes.

2. Place Brie in baking dish and heat in oven during last 8 minutes garlic bakes (Brie should be slightly melted).

3. Arrange toasted bread, roasted garlic halves, and baked Brie on a large serving board. To serve dig out baked garlic clove and spread on a slice of toast, then scoop up some Brie and spread on top of garlic.

Serves 4 to 6

• ACORN SQUASH BISQUE •

In the cool months, when pumpkins are available, serve this soup in a hollowed pumpkin shell. Calico Cornmeal Scones make a particularly nice accompaniment.

2 large acorn squash (about 2 lb), halved and seeded	2 teaspoons minced fresh marjoram *or* ½ teaspoon crushed dried marjoram
2 large leeks (white part only), washed well and cut into ¼-inch slices	¾ teaspoon salt
	⅛ teaspoon white pepper
3 tablespoons unsalted butter	2 cups half-and-half
4 cups rich chicken stock (preferably homemade)	2 tablespoons fresh lemon juice
	¼ teaspoon hot-pepper sauce
1 tablespoon tomato paste	Snipped chives or chopped fresh dill, for garnish
1 bay leaf	

1. Preheat oven to 350° F. Place squash, cut side down, in a baking dish with ½ inch water; bake until tender (about 35 minutes). Or, cook in microwave oven at 100 percent power 10 to 12 minutes.

2. In a large stockpot over medium heat, sauté leeks in butter until translucent (about 5 minutes), stirring occasionally. Scoop out squash pulp and add to leeks. Add chicken stock, tomato paste, bay leaf, marjoram, salt, and pepper. Simmer 20 minutes. Remove from heat and discard bay leaf.

3. In a food processor or blender, purée soup in several batches and return to pan. Blend in half-and-half and heat through; do not boil.

4. Stir in lemon juice and hot-pepper sauce. Taste and add additional salt if needed. Serve garnished with chives or dill.

Serves 6

• CALICO CORNMEAL SCONES •

These scones are a contemporary version of a traditional tea food. Bits of green onion and red bell pepper add lively color; cornmeal adds crunch.

1½ cups sifted flour	2 tablespoons thinly sliced green onion
¾ cup cornmeal	3 tablespoons diced red bell pepper
4 teaspoons baking powder	1 egg
½ teaspoon baking soda	½ to ⅔ cup buttermilk
½ teaspoon salt	1 egg mixed with 1 tablespoon water, for egg wash
½ cup unsalted butter, chilled and cut into pieces	
3 tablespoons vegetable shortening, cut into pieces	

1. Preheat oven to 400° F. In a large mixing bowl, combine flour, cornmeal, baking powder, baking soda, and salt.

2. With a pastry blender cut in butter and shortening until mixture resembles coarse meal. Stir in green onion and red bell pepper.

3. Beat together egg and ½ cup buttermilk. Add to flour mixture and stir with a fork, adding more buttermilk if needed to form a soft dough. Turn dough out onto lightly floured surface and knead 8 to 10 times.

4. Roll out dough ½ inch thick; cut into rounds with a 2-inch biscuit cutter or cut into squares with a sharp knife. Brush tops with egg wash. Place on greased baking sheets and bake until light golden brown (about 20 minutes).

Makes 12 to 18 scones, depending on size

• CORN RELISH •

An old family favorite, this relish is a delicious accompaniment to roast beef and a nice side dish with meat sandwiches. Most specialty produce markets will offer bell peppers in several colors.

2 cups distilled white vinegar	4 cups corn kernels (cut from 9 to 10 ears fresh corn)
½ cup water	2 cups shredded cabbage
½ to 1 cup sugar, to taste	1 red bell pepper, diced
2 tablespoons salt	1 green bell pepper, diced
1 teaspoon celery seed	1 yellow bell pepper, diced
2 teaspoons mustard seed	1 cup diced onion
2 teaspoons turmeric	

1. In a large stockpot, combine vinegar, the water, sugar, salt, celery seed, mustard seed, and turmeric. Cook over low heat, stirring, until sugar is dissolved. Add corn and simmer 5 minutes.

2. Add cabbage, bell peppers, and onion; simmer over low heat 20 minutes. Increase heat to medium-high and bring to a boil.

3. Immediately pack relish in hot sterilized jars, leaving ¼ inch headspace. Seal and process in hot water bath 10 minutes.

Makes 4 to 5 pints

• SOUTHERN BOURBON CAKE •

This holiday recipe works well as part of a dessert buffet. Note that the raisins must soak in the bourbon for a day. The cake will taste even better if allowed to age a few days before serving, which makes this do-ahead recipe ideal for entertaining.

2 cups golden raisins	1 cup unsalted butter, softened
1 cup bourbon	2 teaspoons grated nutmeg or mace
2 cups sifted flour	2 cups sugar
1 teaspoon baking powder	6 eggs, separated
½ teaspoon salt	1 pound pecan halves

1. Soak raisins in bourbon 24 hours. Preheat oven to 325° F. Sift together flour, baking powder, and salt; set aside.

2. In a large mixing bowl, beat butter to soften. Add nutmeg and 1½ cups of the sugar; beat until mixture is fluffy. Add egg yolks and beat 2 minutes, scraping bowl several times while mixing.

3. Add one third of the sifted dry ingredients to creamed butter and mix to blend. Stir in raisins and bourbon. Add remaining dry ingredients and mix just enough to incorporate. Stir in nuts.

4. In a separate bowl beat egg whites until they hold soft peaks. Gradually mix in the remaining ½ cup sugar and beat until whites are stiff but not dry. Fold egg whites into cake batter, one third at a time.

5. Turn batter into a greased and floured 12-cup bundt pan. Bake until a cake tester inserted into center of cake comes out clean (about 1½ hours). Let cake cool for 30 minutes. Turn out on rack and allow to cool completely.

6. Wrap cake airtight and refrigerate for a day or two before eating. To serve slice thinly with a sharp knife.

Serves 8 to 10

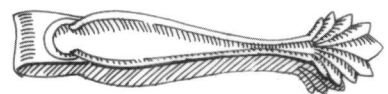

Winter Cream Tea
Serves 12

Piled in a delicate silver filigree basket on the cloth-covered tea cart is a batch of currant-studded scones. These flaky rolls are especially delicious with homemade marmalade. The recipe for Currant Scones is on page 37. Apple-Ginger Marmalade can be found on page 38.

Cream Sherry
Cheese Wafers
Mushroom Tarts
Currant Scones With Mock Devonshire Cream
Apple-Ginger Marmalade
Grannie's Shortbread
Chocolate Truffle Fruit Tarts
Yunnan or Pingsuey Tea

In England a winter tea is hearty, and when served with cream, it becomes a cream tea. Devonshire cream, a rich clotted cream from Devonshire, is usually served with scones but may also be served with strawberries and other fruits. This cream is rare outside of England. Some specialty food shops may import it in small amounts. Tarts are always appropriate for tea because they are easily eaten in one or two bites. A lemon curd version is perhaps the best known. This menu includes two tart recipes—one savory and one sweet. Marmalades and preserves are also a part of traditional tea fare, generously spread on biscuits, scones, crumpets, and muffins.

• CHEESE WAFERS •

These peppery, crispy wafers are extremely easy to prepare and will disappear quickly. For a light snack, serve them with fruit and a glass of port.

1 cup margarine, softened	1 teaspoon Worcestershire sauce
1 cup grated sharp Cheddar cheese	1¼ cups flour
¾ cup cornmeal	1½ tablespoons diced green chile

1. In a large bowl cream margarine and cheese together. Add cornmeal, Worcestershire sauce, flour, and chile; mix thoroughly. Chill dough 1 hour.

2. Preheat oven to 300° F. To form wafers pinch off pieces of dough the size of cherries. Roll into balls. Place on ungreased baking sheet and flatten each ball with bottom of a glass. Bake until golden brown (30 to 35 minutes).

Makes 6 dozen wafers

• MUSHROOM TARTS •

Use either miniature muffin tins or tart pans to prepare these savory, herb-seasoned tarts. Both types of pans are available at better cookware stores. The little tart pans can be unstable; to more easily transport them from counter to oven and then from oven to cooling rack, set the pans on a baking sheet.

¼ cup vegetable oil	1 tablespoon minced fresh marjoram *or* 1½ teaspoons crushed dried marjoram
½ cup butter	
1 pound mushrooms, finely chopped	
½ cup finely chopped parsley	½ cup freshly grated Parmesan cheese
⅓ cup finely chopped green onions (include some of the green tops)	¾ cup dry bread crumbs
½ teaspoon salt	Cream Cheese Pastry Shells (see opposite page)
¼ teaspoon freshly ground pepper	

1. In a large skillet heat oil and butter. Sauté mushrooms, parsley, and green onion 5 minutes, stirring constantly.

2. Remove from heat and add salt, pepper, marjoram, cheese, and bread crumbs. Mix thoroughly and cool for 1 hour.

3. Fill unbaked tart shells. (Tarts may be frozen at this point. Cover with plastic wrap and then aluminum foil and freeze unbaked.) If baking right away, bake in a preheated 350° F oven until filling bubbles and pastry is light-brown (15 to 20 minutes). For frozen tarts, defrost 1 hour at room temperature and bake in a preheated 350° F oven 20 to 25 minutes.

Makes 24 miniature tarts

Cream Cheese Pastry Shells

3 ounces cream cheese, softened	1 cup flour
½ cup butter or margarine, softened	¼ teaspoon salt

Mix cream cheese and butter together. Add flour and salt; mix well. Chill dough 1 hour. Divide dough into twenty-four 1-inch balls. Place balls in miniature muffin tins or in tiny tart pans, pressing dough into sides and bottoms. Cover and chill while preparing filling. For unfilled, baked tart shells, bake them in a preheated 400° F oven until lightly brown on edges (10 to 15 minutes).

Makes 24 miniature tart shells

• CURRANT SCONES •

The dough should be slightly sticky. If dry, add 1 to 2 tablespoons more buttermilk. A sticky dough produces a lighter final product. For a decorative touch, shape the scones with a scalloped or heart-shaped cutter.

3 cups sifted flour	½ cup butter, slightly chilled
3 tablespoons sugar	½ cup dried currants
2 tablespoons baking powder	1 cup buttermilk
¼ teaspoon salt	

1. Preheat oven to 375° F. Into a large mixing bowl, sift flour, sugar, baking powder, and salt. With a pastry blender cut in butter until mixture resembles coarse meal. Stir in currants.

2. Make a well in center. Pour in buttermilk and stir with a fork to blend into rough dough. Turn out onto a lightly floured surface and knead 8 to 10 times until a smooth dough is formed.

3. Roll out dough ½ inch thick. Cut into rounds with a biscuit cutter or cut into squares with a sharp knife.

4. Bake on greased baking sheets until barely brown on top (15 to 20 minutes). Don't overbake or they will be dry.

Makes 24 to 36 scones, depending on size

• MOCK DEVONSHIRE CREAM •

Clotted cream is not readily duplicated in the United States. This recipe comes close, however. Serve with scones and jam or fresh fruit.

½ cup whipping cream	½ cup sour cream
2 tablespoons confectioners' sugar	

In a chilled bowl beat cream until medium-stiff peaks form, adding sugar during last few minutes of beating. Fold in sour cream and blend.

Makes 1½ cups

• APPLE-GINGER MARMALADE •

Try this spicy spread as an accompaniment to ham. For an unusual sandwich filling, chop 2 to 3 tablespoons of the marmalade and blend with 3 ounces cream cheese. This marmalade may also be made with pears instead of apples.

7 cups sugar	½ cup diced candied lemon peel
2 cups water	12 cups diced apples (10 to 12 large apples)
Rind of 1 lemon, grated	
Rind of 1 orange, grated	1 tablespoon minced fresh ginger
½ cup diced candied ginger	1 package (3 oz) liquid fruit pectin

1. In a large nonaluminum saucepan, combine sugar and water. Bring to a boil, reduce heat, and simmer 5 minutes.

2. Add citrus rinds, candied ginger, candied lemon peel, apples, and ginger. Simmer until apples are tender but not mushy (about 35 minutes). Remove from heat and add pectin, stirring 1 minute. Stir with metal spoon and skim foam from top.

3. Ladle into sterilized jars. Seal and process in hot water bath for 5 minutes.

Makes 10 to 12 half-pints

• GRANNIE'S SHORTBREAD •

My cooking assistant, Marilyn Smith, offers this shortbread recipe, which she received from her mother, Eleanor Innes. Each Christmas Marilyn gives the Gentry family a gift of her homemade shortbread, which is always consumed with great pleasure and disappears quickly.

½ cup sugar	2 cups flour
½ cup cornstarch	1 cup butter, melted

1. Preheat oven to 300° F. Sift sugar, cornstarch, and flour together. Mix in butter. Knead slightly; press into two 8-inch round cake pans. Prick all over with a fork.

2. Bake until set but not browned (30 to 40 minutes). Remove from oven and score into wedges. Allow to cool in pan.

Makes about 16 wedges

• CHOCOLATE TRUFFLE FRUIT TARTS •

These tarts, which lusciously combine the richness of chocolate candy with the sweet refreshment of fresh fruit, are a colorful addition to a plate of assorted cookies and pastries. Vary the fruit toppings for added appeal.

- 6 ounces semisweet chocolate chips
- 1 tablespoon butter
- ⅓ cup sugar
- 1 tablespoon half-and-half
- 1 teaspoon coffee-, orange-, cherry-, or raspberry-flavored liqueur
- 1 egg, at room temperature
- ⅓ cup finely chopped toasted pecans or walnuts
- 1 recipe unbaked Cream Cheese Pastry Shells (see page 37)
- Fresh fruits (choose fruits that complement the choice of liqueur—mandarin oranges, fresh cherries, strawberries, or raspberries), for garnish (optional)
- Apricot Glaze (see below), optional
- Strawberry Glaze (see below), optional

1. Preheat oven to 350° F. In a double boiler over hot (not boiling) water, melt chocolate chips and butter. Add sugar, half-and-half, liqueur, and egg; beat until smooth. Stir in nuts.

2. Place one rounded teaspoon of filling into each pastry shell. Bake until filling is set (20 to 25 minutes). Cool in pans 15 minutes. Transfer to wire racks and let cool completely.

3. If desired, decorate tops of tarts with fresh fruit of choice and glaze with appropriate glaze: apricot for light fruits and strawberry for dark fruits.

Makes 24 tarts

Apricot Glaze

- 1 jar (12 oz) apricot jam
- 1 or 2 tablespoons brandy or fresh lemon juice

In a small saucepan over low heat, melt jam. Remove from heat and strain into bowl; blend in brandy. Cool to lukewarm before applying.

Makes 1 cup

Strawberry Glaze

- 1 package (10 oz) frozen strawberries in sugar syrup
- ½ cup currant jelly
- 1 tablespoon cornstarch
- 1 tablespoon cold water

In a small, heavy-bottomed saucepan over medium-high heat, bring berries and jelly to a boil. Combine cornstarch and water and add to berry mixture. Cook 1 minute, stirring constantly. Strain into bowl and cool to lukewarm.

Makes 1⅓ cups

VALENTINE'S DAY TEA
Serves 12

Blanc de Noir Champagne
Cucumber Hearts
Smoked Salmon Hearts
Asparagus Rolls
Cherry Tomatoes, With Shrimp Filling
Chocolate Date-Nut Bread
Coeur à la Crème With Berries
Viennese Sandwich Cookies
Coconut-Raspberry Madeleines
Black Currant Tea

Hearts and strawberries add appropriate color and shape to a tea in honor of Valentine's Day. Although strawberries are expensive in February, the appeal they add is worth the expense. If you collect antique silver, a set of strawberry forks would make a lovely addition and would be very appropriate to use when serving the Coeur à la Crème.

For a small group that can be seated, present this menu in two courses; serve the sandwiches, Asparagus Rolls, and stuffed tomatoes first, then the sweets. Prepare the cherry tomatoes for stuffing by removing the tops and scooping out the pulp with a small melon baller or tomato corer. The Shrimp Filling recipe (see page 21) is included in the section on tea sandwiches.

This menu is also suitable for a summer meal. Use summer fruits to accompany the Coeur à la Crème. The heart-shaped sandwiches are charming any time, or, if you prefer, they can be cut in rounds.

Photograph, page 42: Heart-shaped Coeur à la Crème, a sweet molded cheese dessert, is the centerpiece of a charming tea in honor of Valentine's Day. To carry out the theme, offer cookie hearts and luscious red strawberries. On the table, next to the plate of berries, is an antique strawberry fork.

• CUCUMBER HEARTS •

Cucumbers are a crisp counterpoint to the creamier fillings of the other sandwiches. The mayonnaise both adds flavor and prevents the bread from getting soggy.

1 loaf thin-sliced white sandwich bread	1 cucumber (large enough in diameter that hearts may be cut from the slices)
¼ cup Watercress Mayonnaise (see page 21)	Watercress leaves or edible flowers, for garnish

1. Using a 2-inch heart-shaped cookie cutter, cut heart-shaped bread slices for the sandwich bases. Spread a light coating of mayonnaise on each bread slice.

2. Peel and slice cucumber; cut each slice into a heart with the cutter. Place cucumber hearts on top of bread hearts. Garnish each sandwich with a very small dab of mayonnaise topped with a watercress leaf or an edible flower.

Makes 18 to 24 sandwiches

• SMOKED SALMON HEARTS •

If you feel like splurging, buy 6 to 8 ounces of smoked salmon. With the heart-shaped cookie cutter, cut out heart-shaped pieces of salmon. Use leftover salmon for the Smoked Salmon Spread.

24 slices thin-sliced white sandwich bread	2 ounces smoked salmon, cut in small pieces, for garnish
Smoked Salmon Spread (see below)	Dill sprigs, for garnish

Using a 2-inch heart-shaped cookie cutter, cut out hearts from bread slices for the sandwich bases. Cover bread hearts with salmon spread. Top with a piece of smoked salmon and a sprig of dill.

Makes 24 sandwiches

Smoked Salmon Spread

6 ounces cream cheese, softened	⅓ cup chopped pistachios
3 to 4 ounces smoked salmon, finely chopped	3 to 4 teaspoons fresh lemon juice
	2 to 3 teaspoons snipped fresh dill

Combine all ingredients until smooth.

Makes about 1¼ cups

• ASPARAGUS ROLLS •

The bread will roll more easily when flattened first. Daikon radish sprouts are larger than the more common mung bean sprouts and have a refreshing, peppery bite.

24 slices thin-sliced white sandwich bread, crusts removed
⅓ cup unsalted butter
½ cup Watercress Mayonnaise (see page 21)
24 thin slices boiled ham (optional)
24 asparagus spears, cooked until tender-crisp
Daikon radish sprouts, for garnish

1. With rolling pin, flatten bread slices. Spread each bread slice with a thin layer of butter and mayonnaise.

2. Place slices of ham, if using, on bread, then lay an asparagus spear and some sprouts (let sprouts extend beyond bread) along one edge of bread. Roll bread around spear and sprouts. Serve immediately. If storing for a short time, arrange Asparagus Rolls on tray and cover tightly with plastic wrap.

Makes 24 sandwiches

• CHOCOLATE DATE-NUT BREAD •

Dates make this rich quick bread especially moist, so it will keep well. Nut breads slice better the day after baking, so prepare this recipe in advance.

1 cup boiling water
1 cup chopped dates
¼ cup butter or margarine
1 cup sugar
1 egg
1 teaspoon vanilla extract
2 ounces unsweetened chocolate, melted
2 cups sifted flour
½ teaspoon salt
1 teaspoon baking soda
⅔ cup chopped pecans
Cream Cheese Filling (see below)

1. Pour the boiling water over dates. Set aside and cool to lukewarm.

2. In a large mixing bowl, cream together butter, sugar, egg, and vanilla until light and fluffy. Stir in chocolate.

3. Sift together flour, salt, and baking soda; blend in chopped nuts. Alternately add dry ingredients and date mixture to creamed mixture, mixing well after each addition.

4. Turn batter into greased 9- by 5-inch loaf pan. Bake in a preheated 350° F oven 1 hour, or until done when tested with a toothpick. Cool in pan 10 minutes. Turn out of pan and finish cooling on a baking rack. To serve slice bread; spread half the slices with Cream Cheese Filling. Cover with remaining slices and cut into small pieces.

Serves 8

Cream Cheese Filling

1 package (8 oz) cream cheese, softened
2 tablespoons whipping cream

Combine softened cream cheese with whipping cream.

Makes about 1 cup

• COEUR À LA CRÈME WITH BERRIES •

Shaped in a traditional heart-shaped, white porcelain mold with perforated bottom, *coeur à la crème* is particularly suited for Valentine's Day. Chill overnight before serving. Classically, this is a sweet dish, and thought of as a dessert. However, the preparation works equally well as a savory starter when flavored with herbs and spread on bread or crackers (see Herbed Coeur à la Crème, page 104).

1 pint cottage cheese	3 egg whites
4 ounces cream cheese, softened	Raspberry Sauce (see below)
4 tablespoons confectioners' sugar	1 pint strawberries, rinsed and
1 teaspoon vanilla extract	patted dry (stems left on),
1 cup whipping cream	for garnish

1. Line 1 large coeur à la crème mold with dampened cheesecloth cut large enough to generously hang over sides; set aside.

2. Combine cottage cheese and cream cheese. Add sugar and vanilla and mix thoroughly. Whip cream until medium-soft peaks form, and fold in. Whip egg whites until stiff, but not dry, and fold in.

3. Fill mold with mixture and fold cheesecloth over top. Place mold on a rack over a shallow pan; refrigerate at least 24 hours to allow whey to drain. To serve, unmold onto serving plate; surround with Raspberry Sauce and strawberries.

Serves 12

Raspberry Sauce

1 package (10 oz) frozen raspberries in sugar syrup, thawed	2 tablespoons cold water
½ cup currant jelly	1 tablespoon cornstarch

In a medium, heavy-bottomed saucepan, bring raspberries and jelly to a boil. Combine cold water and cornstarch and whisk into raspberry mixture. Cook 1 minute, stirring constantly. Cool and strain through fine sieve.

Makes 1½ cups

• VIENNESE SANDWICH COOKIES •

Apply the frosting in a thin layer. If too much frosting is used, it will ooze out from between the cookie layers when eaten. Any shape of cookie cutter can be used to form the layers, but a heart cutter is always appealing—especially on Valentine's Day.

- ¾ cup pecans
- ¾ cup sugar
- ¾ cup butter, softened
- 2 cups sifted flour
- 2 tablespoons instant chocolate-drink mix
- 1 tablespoon whipping cream
- 1 teaspoon vanilla extract
- 1 teaspoon rum extract
- Chocolate Frosting (see below)
- Raspberry preserves, for filling
- Confectioners' sugar, for dusting

1. In food processor with metal blade, combine pecans and sugar until pecans are finely chopped and mixture is blended.

2. In a large bowl beat butter and flour together until smooth. Blend in pecan mixture, chocolate-drink mix, cream, vanilla, and rum extract. Form dough into a ball; chill 20 minutes.

3. Preheat oven to 350° F. On a lightly floured surface, roll out dough ⅛ inch thick. Cut an even number of shapes with cookie cutter. With a small canapé cutter cut out the center of half the cookies (so when cookies are sandwiched together, the jam will show through).

4. Place on ungreased baking sheets. Bake until lightly browned (8 to 10 minutes). Cool 1 minute, then remove from sheets. Finish cooling on baking racks.

5. To assemble cookie sandwiches, spread a thin layer of frosting on top and bottom pieces. Spread a small amount of raspberry preserves on bottom cookie. Sandwich the bottom and top cookies together. When all sandwich cookies are completed, dust with sifted confectioners' sugar.

Makes 24 to 36 cookies

Chocolate Frosting

- ½ cup semisweet chocolate chips
- 2 tablespoons whipping cream
- 1 tablespoon butter
- ½ teaspoon rum extract
- ⅓ cup sifted confectioners' sugar

In a double boiler over simmering water, melt chocolate chips with cream, stirring constantly. Remove from heat. Stir in butter, rum extract, and sugar until smooth. If frosting is thin, place in refrigerator for several minutes to harden slightly; remove when of desired spreading consistency.

Makes about ¾ cup

• COCONUT-RASPBERRY MADELEINES •

In this delicious variation of a classic French cookie, a coconut-flavored batter surrounds a sweet raspberry jam filling. Madeleine pans are tinned-steel trays with distinctive shell-shaped molds; they are available at well-stocked cookware stores. If desired, apricot jam can be substituted for the raspberry.

1 cup unsalted butter, softened	½ teaspoon vanilla extract
2½ cups sifted confectioners' sugar	¼ cup finely grated unsweetened coconut
4 large eggs, at room temperature	
2 cups unbleached flour	¼ cup raspberry jam
Pinch salt	Confectioners' sugar, for dusting
½ teaspoon lemon extract	

1. Preheat oven to 350° F. Lightly coat madeleine pans with vegetable cooking spray. With electric mixer cream butter until smooth. Gradually add sugar and beat until fluffy. Add eggs, one at a time, beating well after each addition. Sift together flour and salt; gradually add flour mixture to butter mixture and mix thoroughly. Add lemon and vanilla extracts and coconut and mix well.

2. Fit pastry bag with a large, plain tip and fill with batter; pipe approximately 1½ teaspoons batter into each madeleine mold.

3. Whip jam to liquefy. Place ¼ teaspoon jam on top of the piped batter of each madeleine, smoothing with the back of a spoon to distribute a thin layer of jam across the surface of batter. Pipe approximately 1½ teaspoons batter over the jam on each madeleine to enclose and cover it.

4. Bake until lightly browned (15 to 17 minutes). Remove from oven and immediately turn out onto rack to cool. Lightly dust with confectioners' sugar.

Makes 3 dozen cookies

BRIDAL SHOWER
Serves 8

Raspberry Champagne Punch
Endive Spears With Duck Liver and Forest Mushroom Pâté
Cream Puffs With Egg-Olive Filling and Shrimp Filling
Three Breads: Peanut Butter, Pineapple, and Trumps Dill
The Weyburn Salad Plate
Assorted Pastel Mints
Sugared Nuts (see page 138)
Cinnamon Pastry Spirals
Lemon Raspberry Charlotte
Chardonnay or Sparkling White Zinfandel
China Rose Tea

During my career as assistant manager of the Lotus Tearoom at Bullock's Westwood, a Los Angeles department store, I was also party coordinator. For special events I drew from our regular menus and added a dash of creativity so that each party was unique, a necessity since we had so many customers who regularly entertained at the tearoom for the same group of friends.

I have built this menu around The Weyburn Salad Plate. This dish was designed for the Bullock's Westwood menu (Weyburn is the name of the street where the store is located). It consists of three lettuce cups—one filled with fresh fruits in season, the second with custard, and the third with chicken salad. It is a beautiful plate and especially appropriate for a bridal shower luncheon, baby shower, or birthday celebration.

The tea breads and cream puffs can be made ahead and frozen; the savory fillings, pâté, chicken salad, and desserts can be made the day before. At the tearoom we also used the chicken salad as a filling for tea sandwiches.

• RASPBERRY CHAMPAGNE PUNCH •

This light, refreshing, sparkling punch is not too sweet. It has a soft pink color from the raspberry purée and the Champagne that will enhance a pastel table decor.

- 1 cup white grape juice
- 1 package (10 oz) frozen raspberries, thawed
- ¼ cup raspberry liqueur, brandy, or kirsch
- 2 tablespoons fresh lime juice
- 1 bottle (750 ml) pink Champagne

In a blender or food processor, combine grape juice and raspberries. Strain to remove seeds. Pour mixture into punch bowl. Add liqueur and lime juice; stir to combine. Slowly pour in Champagne.

Makes sixteen 3-ounce servings

• ENDIVE SPEARS WITH DUCK LIVER AND FOREST MUSHROOM PÂTÉ •

Cornichons are small French pickles available at specialty food stores. They are a traditional pâté accompaniment. Crackers or baguette slices can be substituted for the endive spears, if desired. Note that the pâté must chill overnight to firm. This recipe easily doubles for a larger party.

- ½ pound duck livers, trimmed
- 2 tablespoons butter
- 2 tablespoons red wine
- 1 teaspoon salt
- ½ teaspoon freshly ground pepper
- 1 tablespoon minced fresh thyme
- 1½ teaspoons minced garlic
- 6 ounces fresh oyster or shiitake mushrooms
- 8 ounces cream cheese, softened
- Belgian endive spears, for accompaniment
- Sliced cornichons and chopped red onion, for garnish

1. In a large, heavy-bottomed skillet over medium heat, cook duck livers in butter until no longer pink (10 to 15 minutes). Add red wine, salt, pepper, thyme, and garlic; add mushrooms and cook until tender (about 5 minutes).

2. In a food processor fitted with a steel blade, purée duck liver mixture until smooth; add cream cheese and blend until smooth.

3. Line a 4-cup mold with plastic wrap. Spread pâté mixture evenly in bowl, pressing firmly to remove all air bubbles. Chill overnight or until firm.

4. To serve, spread a small amount of pâté on lower portion of endive spears and garnish with cornichons and red onion.

Makes about 2 cups pâté, 6 to 8 servings

CREAM PUFFS WITH EGG-OLIVE FILLING AND SHRIMP FILLING

Cream puffs are wonderful for entertaining because they can be made ahead and frozen. Refresh puffs in a 350° F oven for 3 minutes. Both of these fillings can be used several ways: in cream puffs as in this recipe; in tea sandwiches; and as stuffing for vegetables such as cooked new potatoes, cherry tomatoes, or endive leaves.

- 1 cup water
- ½ cup butter
- 1 cup sifted flour
- ¼ teaspoon salt
- 4 eggs, at room temperature
- Egg-Olive Filling (see page 20)
- Shrimp Filling (see page 21)

1. Preheat oven to 400° F. In a medium saucepan over medium-high heat, bring the water and butter to a rolling boil. Reduce heat to medium, add flour and salt together, and cook, stirring, until dough forms a ball and looks like cornmeal mush (about 30 seconds). Remove from heat and cool 2 minutes.

2. Add eggs, one at a time, beating well after each addition. With two teaspoons form dough into rounds and set on 2 parchment-lined baking sheets.

3. Bake 25 to 30 minutes. Turn off oven and let cream puffs dry out in oven as it cools.

4. To serve cut cream puffs in half. Fill half the cream puffs with Egg-Olive Filling and half with Shrimp Filling.

Makes 24 miniature cream puffs

The Weyburn Salad Plate, which consists of chicken salad, fresh fruit, and vanilla custard, is the main course at a tea in honor of the bride. Shown with the salad are Cinnamon Pastry Spirals. Recipes for the complete menu begin on page 49.

• PEANUT BUTTER BREAD •

Serve this delicious loaf to peanut butter lovers. Even aficionados will be challenged to identify the main ingredient. If you decide to use sunflower seeds, you will find them in most supermarkets.

- ¾ cup chunky peanut butter
- ¼ cup butter or margarine
- 1 egg
- 1 tablespoon grated orange rind
- 2 cups sifted flour
- ½ cup sugar
- 1½ teaspoons baking powder
- 1 teaspoon salt
- ½ teaspoon baking soda
- 1 cup milk
- ½ cup chopped nuts or unsalted sunflower seeds

1. Preheat oven to 350° F. In a large mixing bowl, cream peanut butter and butter. Add egg and orange rind and mix well.

2. In a large bowl, sift together flour, sugar, baking powder, salt, and baking soda. Alternately add dry ingredients and milk to creamed mixture, beginning and ending with dry ingredients. Stir in nuts.

3. Pour batter into greased and floured 8- by 4-inch loaf pan. Bake until toothpick inserted in the center comes out clean (about 55 minutes). Cool in pan 10 minutes, then turn out onto wire rack and cool completely.

Serves 8

• PINEAPPLE BREAD •

For a tropical touch substitute 3 tablespoons chopped macadamia nuts for the sesame seed. This moist bread keeps well. Toast the sesame seed by tossing in an ungreased skillet until it begins to color.

- 2½ cups sifted flour
- ⅔ cup sugar
- 4 teaspoons baking powder
- 1¼ teaspoons salt
- ¼ teaspoon ground mace or nutmeg
- ½ cup toasted wheat germ
- 1 large egg, beaten
- ¼ cup vegetable oil
- 1 can (7¾ oz) crushed pineapple, with syrup
- ½ cup milk
- ½ teaspoon grated lemon rind
- 1 tablespoon toasted sesame seed, for topping

1. Preheat oven to 350° F. Sift flour, sugar, baking powder, salt, and mace into a mixing bowl. Stir in wheat germ.

2. Add beaten egg, oil, pineapple (with syrup), milk, and lemon rind. Stir only until dry ingredients are moistened; do not overmix.

3. Turn batter into well-greased 8- by 4- by 3-inch loaf pan. Sprinkle sesame seed over top of batter. Bake until a toothpick inserted in center comes out clean (about 1 hour); test and bake another 10 minutes if needed.

4. Let cool in pan 10 minutes, then turn out onto wire rack and cool completely.

Serves 8

• TRUMPS DILL BREAD •

At Trumps restaurant in Los Angeles, this bread is baked in a Rehrücken or deerback cake pan that produces a half-round loaf, interesting for tea sandwiches. Better cookware stores will probably carry this unusual pan or will be able to order one.

- 2½ cups flour
- ¼ cup sugar
- 3½ teaspoons baking powder
- 1 teaspoon salt
- 1 tablespoon grated orange rind
- ⅔ cup minced dill
- 1 egg
- ¼ cup vegetable oil
- 1¼ cups milk

1. Preheat oven to 350° F. Into a medium bowl, sift flour, sugar, baking powder, and salt. Stir in orange rind and dill. Make a well in center.

2. In a small mixing bowl, beat egg. Slowly whisk in oil and milk. Pour into well and stir to combine. Do not overmix.

3. Pour batter into well-greased and floured 9- by 5-inch loaf pan. Bake until a toothpick inserted in center comes out clean (35 to 40 minutes); test and bake another 5 or 10 minutes if needed.

Serves 8

• THE WEYBURN SALAD PLATE •

On busy days at the Lotus Tearoom, we sometimes served 40 to 50 of these popular salad plates. For a larger group, double the recipe.

- 24 lettuce cups (iceberg or butter lettuce leaves)
- Assorted fresh fruit (cantaloupe, honeydew, watermelon, papaya, strawberries), sliced
- Baked Custard (see below)
- Sweetened whipped cream, for garnish
- 8 whole strawberries, for garnish
- Tearoom Chicken Salad (see below)
- ½ cup toasted sliced almonds
- Honey-Lime Dressing (see below)

For each Weyburn Salad Plate: Arrange 3 lettuce cups on a dinner plate. In first lettuce cup arrange a selection of sliced fresh fruit. In second cup place a square of custard and top with piped whipped cream and a strawberry. Put mound of chicken salad in third lettuce cup and garnish with almonds. Serve with Honey-Lime Dressing.

Serves 8

Baked Custard

- 4 eggs
- ½ cup sugar
- ¼ teaspoon salt
- 3 cups milk, scalded
- ¾ teaspoon vanilla extract
- Few gratings nutmeg

Preheat oven to 350° F. Beat eggs, sugar, and salt together. Slowly beat in scalded milk; add vanilla. Strain into an 8-inch square baking dish. Sprinkle with nutmeg. Place baking dish in a large pan filled with ½ inch of water. Bake until set (45 to 50 minutes). Remove custard from water and place on a rack to cool. Cut into 8 squares.

Serves 8

Tearoom Chicken Salad

- 1 teaspoon chicken-soup base, dissolved in 1 tablespoon hot water
- 1½ to 2½ cups mayonnaise, to taste
- 6 cups cooked white meat chicken, cut into chunks
- 2 tablespoons lemon juice (optional)

Stir soup base into 1½ cups of the mayonnaise, then combine with chicken. Add lemon juice and additional mayonnaise, if desired.

Makes about 8 cups

Honey-Lime Dressing

- 1 cup vegetable oil
- ¾ cup honey
- ¼ cup white wine vinegar
- ¼ cup Rose's Lime Juice
- 1 tablespoon celery seed
- 1 teaspoon paprika
- ¼ teaspoon dry mustard
- ¼ teaspoon salt

Combine all ingredients and mix thoroughly. Store in refrigerator until needed.

Makes 2¼ cups

• CINNAMON PASTRY SPIRALS •

My family has prepared these cinnamon rolls for many years with dough left over from making pie crusts. Tucked in a napkin-lined basket, these spirals are perfect on a brunch buffet table.

- 1 recipe Double Crust Pastry (see page 120)
- ⅔ cup sugar
- 1 tablespoon ground cinnamon
- 6 tablespoons butter, softened

1. Preheat oven to 400° F. Roll out half of dough to a 10- by 14-inch rectangle. In a small bowl combine sugar and cinnamon.

2. Spread dough with half of butter. Sprinkle with half of cinnamon-sugar mixture.

3. Starting with long side roll up dough jelly-roll style. Slice into 1-inch pieces. Repeat with remaining dough, butter, and cinnamon-sugar mixture.

4. Place cinnamon rolls on baking sheet and bake until pastry is light brown (10 to 12 minutes).

Makes 24 to 30 small rolls

• LEMON RASPBERRY CHARLOTTE •

A charlotte is a light and refreshing dessert. This version can be made 1 to 2 days ahead, but add the whipped cream garnish near serving time. If you haven't the time or inclination to prepare your own ladyfingers, buy them from a high-quality bakery.

- Ladyfingers (see opposite page)
- 1 package (10 oz) frozen raspberries in sugar syrup, thawed
- ½ cup currant jelly
- 3 tablespoons cold water
- 2 tablespoons cornstarch
- 1 envelope unflavored gelatin
- ½ cup fresh lemon juice
- 4 eggs, separated and at room temperature
- 1½ cups sugar
- 3 tablespoons butter
- ⅛ teaspoon salt
- Rind of 1 lemon, grated
- 1 teaspoon vanilla extract
- 1 cup whipping cream, whipped
- Raspberry Whipped Cream (see opposite page), for garnish
- ½ cup fresh raspberries, for garnish

1. Line a 9-inch springform pan with Ladyfingers, arranging them upright around the sides and flat in spokes to cover bottom; set pan aside.

2. In a medium, heavy-bottomed saucepan over medium-high heat, bring raspberries and jelly to a boil. Combine cold water and cornstarch and whisk into raspberry mixture. Cook 1 minute, stirring constantly. Cool; strain through fine sieve into a medium bowl and set aside.

3. Soften gelatin in lemon juice and set aside. In a double boiler beat egg yolks; while beating, add 1 cup of the sugar, a small amount at a time, and beat until thick. Add lemon juice–gelatin mixture, butter, and salt to the yolk mixture. Cook, stirring constantly, over hot (not boiling) water, until thick (8 to 10 minutes); remove from heat.

4. Stir in lemon rind and vanilla. Chill in refrigerator or in a bowl of ice, stirring occasionally, until mixture mounds slightly when dropped from a spoon.

5. Beat egg whites until soft peaks form. Gradually add the remaining ½ cup sugar and continue beating until stiff peaks form. Fold egg whites and whipped cream into lemon mixture.

6. Spoon one third of lemon mixture into prepared pan. Spoon a thin layer of raspberry mixture on top. Spoon another third of lemon mixture on top. Repeat layering ending with lemon mixture.

7. Garnish top of charlotte with Raspberry Whipped Cream rosettes; stud each rosette with a fresh raspberry. Chill until firm. Remove sides of springform pan before serving.

Serves 8 to 10

Ladyfingers

3 eggs, separated	1½ teaspoons orange-flower water
6 tablespoons granulated sugar	¼ teaspoon vanilla extract
½ cup sifted cake flour	¼ teaspoon cream of tartar
⅛ teaspoon salt	Confectioners' sugar, for dusting

1. Preheat oven to 325° F. Grease and flour 2 baking sheets. In a medium bowl beat egg yolks with 3 tablespoons of the sugar until very light and thick. Fold in flour and salt until just blended; stir in orange-flower water and vanilla extract.

2. In a medium bowl beat egg whites until foamy. Add cream of tartar and beat until soft peaks form. Gradually mix in remaining 3 tablespoons sugar and beat until stiff peaks form. Quickly and gently fold egg yolk mixture into egg whites.

3. Using a pastry bag with a plain ½-inch round tip, pipe 3-inch fingers of batter onto baking sheets, leaving about an inch of space between the Ladyfingers. Sieve a thin layer of confectioners' sugar over each cookie. Bake until Ladyfingers just begin to turn brown around the edges (12 to 15 minutes). Let cookies sit on baking sheet about a minute to firm and then remove to cool on a rack. For crisper cookies, bake slightly longer (about 3 minutes more).

4. When cool, sprinkle Ladyfingers with additional confectioners' sugar.

Makes about 36 cookies

Raspberry Whipped Cream

| ½ cup whipping cream | 2 tablespoons raspberry liqueur |
| 2 tablespoons sugar | |

Whip cream; gently fold in sugar and raspberry liqueur.

Makes about 1 cup

Teatime Celebrations

A May Day Picnic

Serves 6

Veal Terrine With Mustard Sauce
Watercress Sandwiches
Papaya Stuffed With Crab Salad
Orange Oatmeal Scones
Frangipane Tartlets
Lemon Mint Spritzers
Silver Tip Oolong Tea

Serve this picnic on a special outing or at an outdoor concert. During the summer in the Los Angeles area, many people picnic before concerts at the Hollywood Bowl. Some of the picnic fare is very elaborate, and is occasionally eaten by the light of silver candelabras.

A picnic is a perfect occasion to display and serve foods in colorful baskets. Accessorize in flower-garden colors. If you enjoy picnics, consider stocking up a supply of attractive paper plates and napkins for these occasions; they are pretty to use and simplify cleanup. Brew the tea at home and transport to the picnic site in a thermos. Silver tip oolong also makes delicious iced tea. A piece of ice substitute tucked into the picnic basket will chill perishables until the meal is served.

• VEAL TERRINE WITH MUSTARD SAUCE •

Country-style pâtés and terrines are perfect picnic fare because they are easy to transport and serve. A terrine gets its name from its traditional cooking container.

2 tablespoons unsalted butter	1½ cups fresh bread crumbs
½ pound mushrooms, sliced	(from good-quality French
½ cup finely chopped onion	bread)
(1 small onion)	2 pounds ground veal
2 cloves garlic, minced	⅓ cup minced parsley
2 teaspoons minced fresh thyme	1 teaspoon freshly grated lemon
or marjoram	or orange rind
¼ cup sour cream	Spicy-Sweet Mustard Sauce (see
Salt and freshly ground pepper,	page 96) or baguette slices,
to taste	Dijon-style mustard, and
⅓ cup milk	cornichons (tiny French
2 eggs	pickles), for accompaniment

1. Preheat oven to 350° F. In a medium skillet over medium-high heat, melt butter. Cook mushrooms, onion, and garlic in butter until most of mushroom liquid is evaporated (about 5 minutes). Stir in thyme and sour cream and cook until syrupy (2 to 3 minutes). Season with salt and pepper; set aside.

2. In a large bowl combine milk and eggs. Add bread crumbs; let soak for a few minutes. Add veal, parsley, and lemon rind; mix thoroughly. Season with salt and pepper.

3. Put half of veal mixture into greased 8- by 3-inch loaf pan. Top with mushroom mixture, spreading evenly. Cover with remaining veal mixture, pressing down.

4. Bake 1½ hours. Drain off any fat or juices. To serve warm: Let stand at room temperature 10 minutes. Cut into thick slices and accompany with Spicy-Sweet Mustard Sauce. To serve cold: Cool slightly, then top with a second loaf pan and weight down with canned goods; cool completely. Serve on baguette slices with Dijon-style mustard and cornichons.

Serves 6

• WATERCRESS SANDWICHES •

For an unusual presentation serve these sandwiches, garnished with curly endive and radish roses (see page 125), in a bread basket (see page 22).

Unsalted butter	Watercress Mayonnaise
12 slices thinly sliced white bread,	(see page 21)
crusts removed	2 cups watercress leaves, washed
	well and patted dry

Lightly butter one side of each piece of bread. Spread a generous layer of mayonnaise over the butter. Layer watercress leaves on half the pieces of bread; cover with remaining bread. Cut each sandwich into four triangles.

Makes 24 triangles

• PAPAYA STUFFED WITH CRAB SALAD •

If ripe papayas are unavailable, mound the crab salad in a large pineapple wedge. When cutting pineapple, don't remove leaves; they add a dramatic touch to the sections.

1 cup mayonnaise	1 pound fresh crabmeat, picked over to remove pieces of shell
2 tablespoons fresh lime juice	Salt and white pepper, to taste
1 jalapeño chile, finely minced	3 papayas, peeled, halved, and seeded
¼ cup finely minced cilantro	½ cup toasted slivered almonds, for garnish
3 tablespoons minced green onion (including some of the green tops)	Assorted greens, for garnish

1. In a medium bowl combine mayonnaise, lime juice, jalapeño chile, cilantro, and green onion; stir in crabmeat. Season with salt and pepper, if needed.

2. Spoon crab salad into papaya halves. Serve garnished with toasted almonds on a bed of garden greens.

Serves 6

The English often celebrate good weather by having tea on the lawn. This picnic includes crab salad served in a papaya shell and watercress sandwiches presented in an edible bread basket. Fruit tarts, flavored with fragrant almond paste, make an elegant dessert. The recipes for a May Day Picnic begin on page 56.

• ORANGE OATMEAL SCONES •

These orange-accented biscuits are also perfect for breakfast. You can prepare the dough through step 2, refrigerate overnight, and complete the recipe in the morning.

1½ cups sifted unbleached flour	3 tablespoons unsalted butter, cut in pieces
1½ tablespoons sugar	3 tablespoons vegetable shortening
2½ teaspoons baking powder	⅔ cup plus 1 tablespoon half-and-half
½ teaspoon ground cardamom	Butter and jam or Mock Devonshire Cream (see page 37), for accompaniment
½ teaspoon salt	
½ cup plus 2 tablespoons oatmeal	
2 teaspoons grated orange rind	

1. Preheat oven to 400° F. Into a medium bowl sift flour, sugar, baking powder, cardamom, and salt. Stir in the ½ cup oatmeal and orange rind.

2. With a pastry blender cut in butter and shortening until mixture resembles coarse meal. Make a well in center and pour in the ⅔ cup half-and-half; stir just to moisten dry ingredients. Do not overmix.

3. Turn dough out onto lightly floured surface and knead gently 8 to 10 times.

4. Roll dough ¾ inch thick. Cut out rounds with a biscuit cutter or cut into squares with a sharp knife. Arrange scones on lightly greased baking sheet. Brush tops with remaining half-and-half and sprinkle with the remaining oatmeal.

5. Bake until tops begin to brown slightly (12 to 15 minutes). Do not overbake or scones will be dry. Serve warm with butter and jam, or Mock Devonshire Cream.

Makes 12 to 18 scones, depending on size

• FRANGIPANE TARTLETS •

Now that kiwifruit is being grown in the United States, it has become more affordable. Because the bright green color of kiwifruit is so appealing, I use it often—in desserts, in salads, and as a garnish. Frangipane refers to the almond flavor of the filling.

- 4 ounces almond paste, cut into pieces, at room temperature
- 4 tablespoons sugar
- 2 tablespoons butter, softened
- 2 eggs, lightly beaten
- ½ teaspoon vanilla extract
- ¼ teaspoon almond extract
- 1 teaspoon dark rum
- 1 teaspoon finely grated lemon rind
- 1 recipe unbaked Cream Cheese Pastry Shells (see page 37)
- 4 kiwifruit, peeled and sliced, *or* 1 pint strawberries, stemmed and washed, *or* a combination of both fruits
- Apricot Glaze (see page 39)

1. Preheat oven to 350° F. In food processor combine almond paste and sugar and blend until smooth. Add butter and process. Slowly add eggs, vanilla, almond extract, rum, and lemon rind; process until completely smooth.

2. Scoop 1 teaspoon filling into each pastry shell. Bake until pastry is light brown (about 15 minutes). Cool completely, then remove from tins.

3. Decorate tops of tarts with fruit. Brush with Apricot Glaze.

Makes 24 miniature tarts

• LEMON MINT SPRITZERS •

When I drink these spritzers, I always think of my childhood in Oregon's Willamette River Valley. The recipe was one of my mother's favorites. A few raspberries or a strawberry would add a fresh note to each glass. The syrup may also be used as a sweetener for hot tea or as a marinade for fresh fruit.

- ½ cup sugar
- ½ cup water
- 1 tablespoon finely grated lemon rind
- ¼ cup fresh lemon juice
- ½ cup fresh mint leaves, washed and chopped
- 2 bottles (32 oz each) lemon-lime soda
- Lemon slices and mint leaves, for garnish

1. In a saucepan combine sugar, water, and lemon rind; boil 5 minutes.

2. Remove from heat and stir in lemon juice. Bruise mint to release juice, then add to saucepan and stir. Let mixture sit for several hours; strain.

3. To make spritzers fill tall glasses with ice. Add 2 to 3 tablespoons lemon syrup per glass and fill with soda. Garnish with a lemon slice and fresh mint leaves.

Makes 6 spritzers

High Tea With Asian Flavors
Serves 6

Shao Mai Dumplings
Hot and Spicy Sesame Sauce
Egg Rolls With Vietnamese Dipping Sauce
Chinese Chicken Salad
Zesty Bosc Pears and Gingered Plum Sorbet in Mandarin Cups
Jasmine Tea

Los Angeles has a wonderful collection of gourmet fast-food restaurants. Among my favorites are those specializing in Chinese dim sum, California style. The food at these Asian cafés incorporates the freshest of produce, light sauces, and very little cornstarch.

The flavors are wonderful, redolent of ginger, sesame, garlic, and just enough chile seasoning to spice things up. They are the perfect drop-in spots for the current crop of "foodies" who enjoy nibbling and grazing; in fact their "sum combinations" are designed for sampling small tastes of many dishes. This menu is typical of what you might find at such a place. The Asian ingredients are available at Asian markets or some well-stocked supermarkets.

• SHAO MAI DUMPLINGS •

The trick to these dumplings is in the shaping. The first few times you prepare them, they may not look as perfect as you want. This is an instance where practice will make perfect, however, so keep trying.

- 10 shiitake mushrooms
- ½ pound shrimp, shelled, deveined, and cut into ¼-inch pieces
- ¾ pound coarsely ground lean pork
- 1 teaspoon salt
- 1 teaspoon sugar
- 1½ teaspoons peanut oil
- 2 tablespoons cornstarch
- 1 teaspoon sesame oil
- 1 teaspoon soy sauce
- 1 tablespoon finely minced fresh ginger
- Pinch of white pepper
- 1 package wonton skins

1. Soak mushrooms in warm water 30 minutes; rinse and pat dry. Slice off stems and discard. Slice caps in ¼-inch pieces. In a food processor place mushrooms, shrimp, pork, salt, sugar, peanut oil, cornstarch, sesame oil, soy sauce, ginger, and white pepper. Process by pulsing on and off until mixture is finely minced; do not overprocess, or mixture will be gummy.

2. With kitchen scissors cut wonton skins into 2¼-inch rounds. Place 1 tablespoon filling in middle of each wonton. Place filled wonton in the palm of your hand, holding wonton skin up around the filling. With rounded part of knife handle push wonton skin in folds against the filling, rotating wonton and continuing to form folds. The dumpling will have a basket shape.

3. With knife handle pack down filling. Squeeze dumpling to create a neck. Tap dumpling lightly on work surface to flatten bottom.

4. Place dumplings in steamer and cook 5 to 7 minutes. Serve immediately.

Makes 45 to 50 dumplings

• HOT AND SPICY SESAME SAUCE •

This versatile dipping sauce works well with all types of Asian foods. For an appetizer, serve with romaine spears; dip the lettuce into the sauce.

- 3 large cloves garlic, minced
- 2 to 3 tablespoons minced fresh cilantro (coriander)
- 4 tablespoons Chinese sesame paste, drained of oil
- 1 tablespoon plus 1 teaspoon sesame oil
- 3 tablespoons mushroom soy sauce
- 2 tablespoons dry sherry or Chinese rice wine
- 1 tablespoon rice vinegar
- 1 tablespoon plus 1 teaspoon honey
- ¼ to ½ teaspoon chile oil
- ¼ teaspoon Szechuan Pepper Salt (see opposite page)

In the bowl of a food processor, place garlic, cilantro, sesame paste, sesame oil, soy sauce, sherry, vinegar, honey, chile oil, and ¼ teaspoon Szechuan Pepper Salt. Blend until smooth.

Makes ¾ cup

Szechuan Pepper Salt

1 teaspoon salt   1 tablespoon Szechuan peppercorns

In a small frying pan, combine salt and Szechuan peppercorns; cook over medium heat, shaking pan often until salt begins to brown and peppercorns become fragrant (8 to 10 minutes). Cool mixture. Grind with mortar and pestle or with spice grinder. Strain mixture to remove peppercorn hulls.

Makes 4 teaspoons

• EGG ROLLS WITH VIETNAMESE • DIPPING SAUCE

Fried egg rolls can be wrapped in clean paper towels and refrigerated. Reheat in 400° F oven for 10 minutes. *Nuoc mam* is a Southeast Asian condiment sold at Vietnamese and Thai markets.

- 1 pound lean ground pork
- 1 pound shrimp, finely minced
- ½ cup finely chopped green onion
- 1½ cups bean sprouts, coarsely chopped
- 2 teaspoons sugar
- 1 teaspoon salt
- ½ teaspoon freshly ground pepper
- 1 tablespoon nuoc mam (fish sauce)
- 1 package egg roll wrappers
- 1 egg, beaten
- Oil, for deep-frying
- Vietnamese Dipping Sauce (see below)

1. For filling, in a large bowl combine pork, shrimp, onion, bean sprouts, sugar, salt, pepper, and nuoc mam.

2. To assemble each roll, with your hands shape about 3 tablespoons of filling into a firm cylinder about 4 inches long and 1 inch in diameter. Place cylinder diagonally across lower middle of an egg roll wrapper. Roll lower flap tightly over filling, leaving upper triangle of wrapper exposed. Bring 2 side flaps securely across cylinder, making sure there are no unnecessary wrinkles or looseness in wrapper. It is important to roll each cylinder tightly if you plan to serve egg rolls sliced. Brush exposed triangle with beaten egg. Repeat with remaining filling and egg roll wrappers.

3. In a wok or deep fryer, heat 3 inches of oil to 375° F. Fry 3 or 4 egg rolls at a time. Remove with slotted spoon and drain thoroughly on paper towels. Slice each egg roll into four pieces and serve with dipping sauce.

Makes 48 pieces

Vietnamese Dipping Sauce

- 1 tablespoon plus 2 teaspoons sugar
- 4 cloves garlic, finely minced
- 2 to 4 dried hot chiles, crushed
- 2 teaspoons fresh lime juice
- 5 tablespoons water
- ¼ cup nuoc mam (fish sauce)

In a mixing bowl combine sugar, garlic, and chiles; mash with the back of a spoon or use a mortar and pestle. Add lime juice, water, and nuoc mam; mix thoroughly.

Makes ⅔ cup

• CHINESE CHICKEN SALAD •

Mai fun are Chinese rice flour noodles, available at Asian markets. When fried in oil, the noodles puff dramatically. Use fresh oil (not oil already used for cooking) or the noodles won't expand properly.

1 large whole cooked chicken breast, cooled, skinned, boned, and shredded	2 ounces mai fun noodles *or* 6 wonton wrappers, cut into ¼-inch strips
2 tablespoons soy sauce	1 head iceberg lettuce, shredded
2 tablespoons lightly toasted sesame seed	5 green onions, chopped
Oil, for frying	¼ cup toasted slivered almonds
	Sesame Dressing (see below)

1. In a glass bowl combine shredded chicken with soy sauce and sesame seed; marinate in refrigerator for several hours; let sit at room temperature for about 30 minutes before tossing with other ingredients.

2. In hot oil fry mai fun noodles (or wonton strips) a few at a time; don't crowd pan or let oil temperature drop or noodles won't puff. Drain on paper towels.

3. Put lettuce in a large salad bowl. Top with chicken, fried noodles, and green onions; sprinkle with almonds.

4. Just before serving, whisk dressing and pour over salad. Toss to mix.

Serves 6

Sesame Dressing

2 tablespoons sugar	1 tablespoon sesame oil
1 teaspoon salt	¼ cup vegetable oil
½ teaspoon freshly ground pepper	2 tablespoons chopped fresh cilantro (coriander)
3 tablespoons champagne vinegar	

Combine sugar, salt, pepper, vinegar, sesame oil, vegetable oil, and cilantro.

Makes about ¾ cup

ZESTY BOSC PEARS AND GINGERED PLUM SORBET IN MANDARIN CUPS

Asian menus are complicated to orchestrate because so many of the dishes must be cooked at the last minute. This dessert can be prepared ahead of time and quickly assembled following the main course. I make the pears two days in advance so they can marinate in the flavored syrup. The sorbet and cookie cups can be made the day before. Store the cookie cups in an airtight container.

Vegetable oil, for frying
6 egg roll wrappers (6-inch square)
½ cup confectioners' sugar
½ teaspoon ground ginger
Zesty Bosc Pears (see below)
Gingered Plum Sorbet (see below)

1. In a 1-quart, heavy-bottomed saucepan, heat 3 inches of oil. Fold each wrapper in half and trim into a half-moon shape. Open wrappers. Lower one wrapper at a time into pan, using a soup ladle to push wrapper down into hot oil. Wrapper will flatten against ladle, forming a cup. Fry until golden brown (1 to 1½ minutes). Invert onto paper towels to drain.

2. Combine sugar and ginger and sift over outside of each cookie cup. To serve, place dessert cups on attractive serving plates. Slice pears and place several pieces in each cup. Top with scoops of Gingered Plum Sorbet.

Serves 6

Zesty Bosc Pears

6 whole firm Bosc pears
1 cup sweet sherry
1 cup water
¾ cup light corn syrup
1 piece star anise
1 piece (1½ in.) vanilla bean
¼ cup *each* strips of lemon, lime, and orange rind, cut with a zester
3 tablespoons fresh lemon juice

Peel pears. Remove cores from blossom ends; leave stems attached. In a nonaluminum pan combine sherry, water, corn syrup, star anise, vanilla bean, and citrus rind. Add pears. Simmer, uncovered, until just softened but still firm (20 to 25 minutes). Do not allow pears to become mushy. Remove pan from heat, stir in lemon juice, and let fruit cool. Refrigerate pears in poaching liquid, tightly covered, until ready to serve.

Makes 6 pears

Gingered Plum Sorbet

½ cup dry white wine
⅓ to ½ cup sugar (depending on sweetness of fruit)
2 tablespoons candied ginger *or* 6 slices fresh ginger
8 ripe fresh plums, pitted and cut into pieces
3 tablespoons fresh lemon juice
2 tablespoons grated lemon rind

In a medium saucepan bring wine, sugar, and ginger to a boil, reduce heat, and simmer 5 minutes. Remove from heat. Cool, strain, and chill. In a blender or food processor, purée chilled syrup, plums, lemon juice, and rind. Transfer purée to ice trays or a baking dish and freeze until firm (at least 4 hours or overnight). Just before serving, remove from freezer, soften slightly, and cut into chunks. Blend in food processor until smooth.

Makes 1½ to 2 cups

A tea is an elegant format for a wedding reception. Surrounding the silver punch bowl filled with Apricot Mist Punch are (from left to right): Tiropitas, Bouchées With Smoked Oyster Pâté, Zesty Deviled Eggs With Caviar, Prosciutto-Wrapped Pear Slices, and Salmon Mousse.

Afternoon Wedding Reception
Serves 24

Apricot Mist Punch

Blanc de Noir Champagne

Crudités With Creamy Mint Sauce

Bouchées With Smoked Oyster Pâté

Crab and Sun-Dried Tomato Tarts

Tiropitas

Cream Puffs With Ham Salad Filling and Shrimp Filling

Zesty Deviled Eggs With Caviar

Salmon Mousse

Cheese Board With Assorted Water Biscuits and Breads

Prosciutto-Wrapped Fig or Pear Slices

**Lemon Bread and Strawberry-Pecan Bread
With Assorted Spreads**

Wedding Cake

Coffee

China Rose Tea

This menu has been designed for a small reception of 24 but can easily be expanded for larger groups. These finger foods are light afternoon fare. Provide small china plates appropriate to the table decor for guests to use for their selections, and be sure to have enough servers to keep the party running smoothly.

You will need to make a double recipe of the mint sauce and bake two loaves of each of the tea breads. A recipe has been provided for making the bouchées from prepared puff pastry dough, but because many details need attention, you might prefer to order the bouchées from a good-quality French bakery.

• APRICOT MIST PUNCH •

This light, refreshing beverage is especially nice for receptions, showers, and weddings. The ring of iced fruit adds visual interest as well as chills to the punch. Use fruit that complements the color of the punch, such as peaches, apricots, and orange segments.

- 1 can (46 oz) apricot nectar
- 1 can (46 oz) pineapple juice
- 1 can (12 oz) frozen limeade concentrate, thawed
- 1 cup fresh lemon juice
- 3 bottles (1 qt each) ginger ale
- 1 cup rum or vodka (optional)
- Frozen ring mold of assorted fresh fruits and 2 cups pineapple juice, for icing punch

Combine apricot nectar, pineapple juice, limeade concentrate, and lemon juice. Pour into punch bowl. Stir in ginger ale. Add rum or vodka, if desired, and frozen ring mold.

Makes fifty 4-ounce servings

• CREAMY MINT SAUCE •

This unusual blend of cool mint and hot chile makes a tasty dip for raw and blanched vegetables (see Crudités With Chick-pea Sauce, page 125, for suggested vegetables, their preparation, and presentation). It is also delicious as an accompaniment to lamb—either chops or a roast. The sauce can be made early in the day and stored in the refrigerator until needed. To serve 24 make two recipes.

- 1 cup mint leaves, washed and stems removed
- 1 tablespoon minced onion
- 2 teaspoons minced jalapeño chile
- 1 teaspoon minced fresh ginger
- ½ teaspoon sugar
- Salt, to taste
- 1 tablespoon white wine vinegar
- 1 cup crème fraîche or sour cream

In a blender or food processor, combine all ingredients except crème fraîche; process in on-off bursts until mint is finely chopped. Add crème fraîche and process briefly just to combine.

Makes 1½ cups, serves 12

• BOUCHÉES WITH SMOKED OYSTER PÂTÉ •

A bouchée is a miniature vol-au-vent (puff pastry shell). Other savory fillings that are suitable for these pastries include Egg-Olive Filling (see page 20) and Shrimp Filling (see page 21). For dessert, try several sweet fillings such as Lemon Curd (see page 78) or Orange Curd (see page 79).

- 1 pound puff pastry dough
- 2 eggs, beaten

Smoked Oyster Pâté
(see opposite page)

1. Preheat oven to 450° F. Roll out puff pastry ⅛ inch thick. For each patty shell cut three 3-inch circles with a biscuit cutter. Place the first circle on a baking sheet and brush with beaten egg. Do not let egg drip on sides.

2. Using a slightly smaller cutter, cut out center of second pastry circle to make a ring. Turn this ring over and place it on first pastry circle. Brush with egg.

3. Press smaller biscuit cutter into third pastry circle but do not cut all the way through. Place this pastry on top of ring and brush with egg. Repeat with remaining dough. Bake 10 minutes. Reduce heat to 350° F and bake until golden and dry (20 minutes).

4. With a sharp knife remove indented centers of top circles of pastry. Return shells to oven to dry (about 2 minutes). Remove pastry shells and cool on baking rack.

5. Place pâté in pastry bag fitted with star tip and pipe some of the mixture into each bouchée; top with pastry circle removed in step 4.

Makes 36 bouchées

Smoked Oyster Pâté

- 2 cans (3¾ oz each) smoked oysters, drained
- ½ cup unsalted butter
- 2 tablespoons whipping cream
- 1 tablespoon finely minced fresh thyme
- 1 teaspoon Worcestershire sauce
- ¼ teaspoon hot-pepper sauce
- ¼ teaspoon salt

Pat oysters with paper towels to remove excess oil. Chop oysters in food processor. Add butter, cream, thyme, Worcestershire sauce, hot-pepper sauce, and salt; purée.

Makes approximately 1½ cups

• CRAB AND SUN-DRIED TOMATO TARTS •

Sun-dried tomatoes give an added depth of flavor to these tarts. The tomatoes are sold at most specialty food stores. If you prefer, use shrimp rather than crab.

- ½ cup minced green onion
- 1 tablespoon unsalted butter
- 8 ounces crab meat, bone and cartilage removed
- ⅓ cup sliced sun-dried tomatoes
- 1 package (9 oz) frozen artichoke hearts, cooked according to package directions, well drained, and cut in chunks
- 2 tablespoons minced fresh basil
- 1 recipe unbaked Cream Cheese Pastry Shells (see page 37)
- 1 cup grated fontina cheese
- 3 eggs
- 1¼ cups half-and-half
- ⅛ teaspoon hot-pepper sauce
- Salt and white pepper, to taste

1. Preheat oven to 400° F. In a medium skillet sauté green onion in butter 3 minutes. Distribute green onion, crab, tomatoes, artichoke hearts, and basil evenly among tart shells; then sprinkle with cheese.

2. In a medium bowl combine eggs, half-and-half, and hot-pepper sauce; whisk to blend. Season with salt and pepper. Pour over cheese. Bake until top is golden and custard is set (15 to 20 minutes).

3. Let cool 5 to 10 minutes and serve.

Makes 24 miniature tarts

• TIROPITAS •

These flaky pastries can be prepared up to the point of baking, then tightly wrapped and frozen. Bake frozen pastries 15 to 20 minutes. Note that the filo dough must thaw before it can be used.

- 6 tablespoons unsalted butter
- ¼ cup flour
- 1 cup milk
- 12 ounces feta cheese, crumbled
- ⅛ teaspoon white pepper
- 2 eggs, plus 1 egg yolk
- 1 pound filo dough, thawed according to package directions
- ½ to 1 cup unsalted butter, melted

1. In a 1-quart saucepan melt the 6 tablespoons butter. Stir in flour and cook over low heat several minutes; remove from heat. Slowly whisk in milk. Return to heat and cook until thickened, stirring constantly.

2. Remove from heat and add crumbled cheese and pepper. Add eggs, one at a time, and egg yolk, beating well after each addition. Chill mixture several hours.

3. Preheat oven to 375° F. Unwrap thawed filo sheets. Work with one at a time. Keep unused portion covered with waxed paper and a slightly damp tea towel.

4. Place a sheet of filo on large work surface. Brush entire filo sheet with melted butter. Cut sheet lengthwise into 2-inch-wide strips. Put about 1 teaspoon cheese filling in one corner of strip and fold it over to make a triangle. Fold forward, then to the opposite side, and then forward (as you would a flag). Continue folding until you reach the end of the strip.

5. Place pastry on baking sheet and brush with melted butter. Repeat steps until all filling has been used. Bake pastries until puffed and golden brown (about 10 minutes). Serve hot or cold.

Makes about 60 pastries

• CREAM PUFFS WITH HAM SALAD FILLING AND SHRIMP FILLING •

Although the recipes for this pastry and these fillings are elsewhere in the book, the combination is well-suited for a wedding reception. Cream puffs can be made ahead and frozen.

Cream Puffs (see page 50)
Ham Salad Filling (see page 20)
Shrimp Filling (see page 21)

Cut puffs in half and remove soft insides. Fill half with each filling.

Makes 24 filled appetizer cream puffs

• ZESTY DEVILED EGGS WITH CAVIAR •

I recently purchased an antique glass deviled-egg serving plate with 15 indentations. My guess is that it was designed for an egg-loving cook: 15 deviled egg halves for the plate and the extra half for the cook.

12 hard-cooked eggs, peeled and halved lengthwise
2 teaspoons Dijon-style mustard
1 to 2 teaspoons white wine vinegar
⅓ cup mayonnaise
Salt and freshly ground pepper, to taste
Golden caviar and fresh dill sprigs, for garnish

1. Scoop out egg yolks and place in small mixing bowl. Mash with a fork and combine with mustard, vinegar, mayonnaise, salt, and pepper.

2. Stuff egg whites with prepared yolk mixture. Garnish tops with golden caviar and sprigs of fresh dill.

Makes 24 deviled egg halves

• SALMON MOUSSE •

The mousse is also suitable as a luncheon salad that will serve eight persons nicely. Be sure to allow enough time for the mixture to set—at least 4 hours. Better still, make it the day before you need it.

1½ cups cooked flaked salmon, bones removed
2 hard-cooked eggs, peeled and chopped
½ cup sliced black olives
1 tablespoon minced fresh dill
1 envelope unflavored gelatin
¼ cup cold water
2 cups mayonnaise
Red leaf lettuce, olive slices, pimiento pieces, and halved cucumber slices, for garnish
2 cucumbers, scored and sliced into rounds, for garnish

1. Combine salmon, eggs, olives, and dill; set aside.

2. In a small saucepan soak gelatin in the cold water 5 minutes, then dissolve gelatin mixture over very low heat. Add small amount of mayonnaise to gelatin, stirring constantly, then add this mixture to remaining mayonnaise.

3. Blend mayonnaise mixture with salmon mixture. Spoon into oiled 3-cup fish mold and chill until firm (about 4 hours).

4. To serve arrange a bed of red leaf lettuce on a serving plate. Unmold salmon mousse onto lettuce. Decorate fish with sliced olives for eyes and pimiento for mouth. Arrange halved slices of cucumber on mousse to resemble fish scales. Serve accompanied with cucumber slices.

Serves 24 as part of a buffet

• PROSCIUTTO-WRAPPED FIG • OR PEAR SLICES

Italians have always enjoyed the contrast of salty prosciutto, a dried ham, with sweet fruit. Most commonly, the ham is wrapped around pieces of melon, but here a more unusual pairing is suggested: prosciutto and figs or pears. A dressing made with balsamic vinegar, also Italian, and honey, adds interest.

- 16 figs, quartered, *or* 6 to 8 pears, cored and sliced
- 6 ounces thinly sliced prosciutto
- ⅓ cup balsamic vinegar
- 1 tablespoon honey
- 2 teaspoons minced fresh mint

Wrap fig or pear slices with small pieces of prosciutto. Combine vinegar, honey, and mint. Drizzle over prepared fig or pear slices.

Makes 64 pieces

• LEMON BREAD •

Although this is a quick bread, it is made by the conventional creaming method used for cakes; the result is a finely textured loaf. Let the bread sit a day before eating; it will slice more cleanly. The bread also freezes well. The following spreads are delicious accompaniments: Chutney Cream Cheese (see page 19), Raspberry Butter (see page 21), or cream cheese mixed with chopped crystallized ginger. To serve 24, you will need to make a double recipe.

- ⅓ cup butter or margarine
- 1 cup sugar
- ½ teaspoon lemon extract
- 2 eggs
- 1½ cups sifted flour
- ¾ teaspoon salt
- 1 teaspoon baking powder
- ½ cup milk
- Grated rind and juice of 1 lemon
- ¾ cup chopped walnuts
- ⅓ cup sugar

1. Preheat oven to 350° F. In a large bowl cream together butter and sugar. Add lemon extract and mix well. Add eggs, one at a time, beating well after each addition.

2. Sift together flour, salt, and baking powder. Alternately add dry ingredients and milk to creamed mixture, beginning and ending with dry ingredients.

3. Fold in lemon rind and walnuts. Pour into greased and floured 8- by 4-inch loaf pan. Bake until toothpick inserted in center comes out clean (about 1 hour).

4. In small saucepan combine lemon juice and sugar and bring to a boil. Remove from heat. Pour mixture over lemon bread when it is removed from oven. Cool loaf in pan.

Serves 12 as part of a buffet

• STRAWBERRY-PECAN BREAD •

For a special presentation, slice bread and spread with whipped cream cheese. Lay a row of overlapping strawberry slices down center of each bread slice; serve open-faced. The spreads suggested for Lemon Bread (see opposite page) also pair well with this bread. To serve 24, make a double recipe.

¾ cup butter or margarine
¾ cup sugar
1 teaspoon vanilla extract
4 eggs
2 cups sifted flour
1 cup oatmeal

2 teaspoons baking powder
¾ teaspoon salt
1 cup strawberry preserves
½ cup sour cream
½ cup finely chopped toasted pecans

1. Preheat oven to 350° F. In a large bowl cream butter, sugar, and vanilla together. Add eggs, one at a time, beating well after each addition.

2. In another mixing bowl combine flour, oatmeal, baking powder, and salt.

3. In a small mixing bowl, combine preserves and sour cream.

4. Alternately add dry ingredients and preserve mixture to creamed butter mixture. Stir in pecans.

5. Turn batter into greased 8- by 4-inch loaf pan. Bake for 1 hour; check to see if loaf is done. Continue baking if necessary until inserted toothpick comes out clean.

6. Cool 10 minutes in pan. Turn out and cool completely on baking rack.

Serves 12 as part of a buffet

Tea fare can be more substantial than finger sandwiches and more exotic than jam and crumpets. For this high tea, the American Southwest sets the theme. Shown clockwise from top right: Chicken Posole, Orange and Lemon Curd Tarts and Jalapeño Jelly Thumbprint Cookies, Tender Greens Tossed With Cantaloupe and Avocado, Jalapeño–Blue Cornmeal Muffins, and Spicy Melon Relish.

SOUTHWESTERN JALAPEÑO HIGH TEA
Serves 6

Tender Greens Tossed With Cantaloupe and Avocado
Chicken Posole
Spicy Melon Relish
Jalapeño–Blue Cornmeal Muffins
Orange and Lemon Curd Tarts
Jalapeño Jelly Thumbprint Cookies
Gamay Beaujolais
Lapsang Souchong Tea

Southwestern cuisine is a complex composite of the regional foods of Texas with its southern, Tex-Mex, barbecue, and trail cooking roots; New Mexico and Arizona cooking, influenced by Pueblo Indian, Mexican, and Spanish cuisines; and the increased availability of ingredients from other parts of the country, particularly specialty produce. The result is zesty, spicy, and earthy cooking. Lapsang souchong tea is quite smoky and pairs well with these foods.

TENDER GREENS TOSSED WITH CANTALOUPE AND AVOCADO

Contrasting tastes and textures—mild butter lettuce, peppery watercress, smooth avocado, sweet melon, and crunchy pecans—make this salad particularly appealing.

- 2 heads butter lettuce, well washed, dried, and torn in bite-sized pieces
- 1 bunch watercress, rinsed, dried, and stemmed
- 2 avocados, peeled and diced
- 1 cup diced cantaloupe
- ¾ cup toasted pecan pieces
- Tarragon Vinaigrette Dressing (see below)

In a large salad bowl combine lettuce, watercress, avocado, cantaloupe, and toasted pecan pieces. Toss with dressing.

Serves 6

Tarragon Vinaigrette Dressing

- ⅓ cup safflower oil
- 4 tablespoons olive oil
- 6 tablespoons fresh lemon juice
- 4 tablespoons tarragon wine vinegar
- 2 cloves garlic, minced
- 1 teaspoon dry mustard
- 1 teaspoon celery salt
- ½ teaspoon white pepper
- 1 tablespoon minced fresh tarragon *or* 1 teaspoon crushed dried tarragon
- 2 teaspoons sugar

In a medium bowl, combine ingredients.

Makes about 1½ cups

• CHICKEN POSOLE •

Posole is a colorful southwestern stew. It is a perfect dish for entertaining; guests always enjoy adding the finishing touches at the table. *Masa harina* is a corn flour available at Latin American markets.

- 2½ pounds chicken pieces *or* 3 large boneless chicken breasts, halved
- 2 tablespoons vegetable shortening
- 2 cloves garlic, minced
- ½ cup finely diced onion
- 2 quarts chicken stock
- 3 tablespoons masa harina
- ½ cup cold water
- 1 tablespoon chili powder
- 1 teaspoon brown sugar
- 1 tablespoon crushed dried oregano
- Salt (1½ teaspoons if stock is unsalted, ½ teaspoon if stock is salted)
- ½ teaspoon freshly ground pepper
- 1 can (16 oz) white hominy, drained
- 1 can (16 oz) yellow hominy, drained
- 1 cup shredded Monterey jack cheese, for garnish
- Sour cream, for garnish
- Accompaniments: chunks of avocado, minced cilantro, chopped red onion, chopped radishes, chopped green bell pepper, Mexican-style hot sauce, lime wedges, and hot buttered tortillas

1. In a large skillet sauté the chicken pieces in the shortening until brown on all sides; remove to platter and set aside.

2. Sauté garlic and onion in drippings. Return chicken to pan. Pour in stock and bring to a boil; reduce heat to low.

3. Mix masa harina with the cold water and add to chicken. Add the chili powder, sugar, oregano, salt, and pepper. Cover and simmer 50 minutes. Add white and yellow hominy and cook for 10 minutes.

4. Skim fat from surface and taste for seasoning. (Posole can be made the day before up to this point, then refrigerated. Remove the hardened fat from the surface before reheating.)

5. Serve in soup bowls with some of the liquid. Sprinkle with jack cheese and top with a dollop of sour cream. Pass accompaniments.

Serves 6

• SPICY MELON RELISH •

The coolness of the melon makes a stimulating counterpoint to the hot bite of the chile and the tang of fresh lime juice. Serve it with Chicken Posole (see opposite page), with grilled or roast chicken, or with simply prepared fish. Jicama, a creamy-white root vegetable with a pleasing crunchy texture, is available at specialty produce stores, Latin American markets, and well-stocked supermarkets.

- 1 small onion, finely chopped
- 1 tablespoon oil
- 1 jicama, peeled and cut in ¼-inch dice
- ½ medium cantaloupe, peeled, seeded, and cut in small dice
- ½ medium honeydew, peeled, seeded, and cut in small dice
- ⅓ cup chopped cilantro
- ½ red bell pepper, diced, *or* 2 red jalapeño chiles, minced
- 2 green jalapeño chiles, finely minced
- 3 tablespoons fresh lime juice

1. In a small pan sauté onion in oil; let cool.

2. Combine remaining ingredients, stir in sautéed onion, and refrigerate several hours to blend flavors.

Makes 4 cups

Teatime Celebrations

• JALAPEÑO–BLUE CORNMEAL MUFFINS •

These muffins add zip to the menu with their hot and spicy flavor. They also complement a hearty soup or, with a small amount scooped out from the top, they can be filled with crab or chicken salad. Blue cornmeal is available at specialty food stores.

1 cup blue cornmeal	1 to 2 tablespoons minced
1 cup sifted flour	jalapeño chiles
1 tablespoon sugar	¼ cup minced onion
1 tablespoon baking powder	1 egg
½ teaspoon salt	⅓ cup vegetable oil
	1 cup milk

1. Preheat oven to 375° F. In a medium bowl combine cornmeal, flour, sugar, baking powder, and salt. Stir in the jalapeño chiles and onion. Make a well in center of dry ingredients.

2. In a medium bowl beat egg; slowly beat in oil and then milk. Pour mixture into well and stir just to combine. Pour batter into well-greased miniature muffin tins.

3. Bake until slightly brown (12 to 15 minutes). Remove from tins while still warm. Cool on wire rack.

Makes 24 to 30 miniature muffins

• ORANGE AND LEMON CURD TARTS •

When serving a menu of spicy foods, I like to finish with a citrus dessert to cool the palate. If you prefer, the tarts can be made with only the more traditional lemon curd, or you can serve both lemon and orange tarts. The recipes here allow for leftover curd, because it is so convenient to have on hand for other uses. Curd will keep in the refrigerator up to 2 weeks.

1 recipe baked Cream Cheese Pastry Shells (see page 37)	Sweetened whipped cream and strips of orange and lemon rind, for garnish
Lemon Curd (see below)	
Orange Curd (see opposite page)	

Fill baked tart shells with lemon or orange curd, or fill half the shells with each type of curd. Garnish with whipped cream and strips of rind.

Makes 24 tarts

Lemon Curd

3 eggs, slightly beaten	¾ cup sugar
½ cup fresh lemon juice	¼ cup butter, cut in small pieces
Rind of 1 lemon, grated	

In medium bowl combine eggs and lemon juice; whisk to blend. Strain mixture into a double boiler. Add lemon rind, sugar, and butter. Cook over hot (not boiling) water until thickened (about 10 minutes), stirring occasionally. Cool and refrigerate curd.

Makes 1½ cups

Orange Curd

3 eggs, plus 2 egg yolks
½ cup fresh orange juice
1 tablespoon finely grated orange rind
½ cup sugar
6 tablespoons butter, cut in small pieces
2 tablespoons fresh lemon juice

In medium bowl combine eggs, egg yolks, and orange juice; whisk to blend. Strain mixture into double boiler. Add orange rind, sugar, butter, and lemon juice. Cook over hot (not boiling) water until thickened (about 10 minutes), stirring occasionally. Cool and refrigerate curd.

Makes about 1½ cups

JALAPEÑO JELLY THUMBPRINT COOKIES

Serve jalapeño jelly as an appetizer with crackers and cream cheese. The jelly is also a delicious accompaniment to roasts, chicken, or turkey. If you are short of time, it can be purchased in gourmet stores.

½ cup butter, softened
¼ cup firmly packed light brown sugar
1 egg, separated
½ teaspoon vanilla extract
1 cup sifted flour
¼ teaspoon salt
¾ cup chopped pecans
Jalapeño Jelly (see below)

1. Preheat oven to 350° F. In a medium bowl thoroughly cream together butter, sugar, egg yolk, and vanilla. Sift flour and salt together and add to creamed mixture.

2. Form dough into 1-inch balls. In a small bowl beat egg white. Dip each ball into beaten egg white, then roll in chopped nuts. Place 1 inch apart on ungreased baking sheets. Press thumb gently into center of each ball.

3. Bake until light golden brown (10 to 12 minutes); cool on racks. Fill centers with Jalapeño Jelly.

Makes 2 dozen cookies

Jalapeño Jelly

½ cup ground green bell pepper (1 large pepper)
½ cup ground red bell pepper (1 large pepper)
½ cup ground jalapeño chiles (5 chiles)
6 cups sugar
1½ cups distilled white vinegar
2 packages (3 oz each) liquid pectin

In a 6-quart saucepan combine ground peppers and chiles, sugar, and vinegar; bring to a hard rolling boil and boil 1 minute. Remove from heat and add pectin; mix well. Skim foam from surface with metal spoon. Pour into hot, sterilized jars. Wipe edge of jars with a clean cloth. Seal jars with canning lid and screw top. Process in a hot water bath for 5 minutes.

Makes 6 to 7 half-pint jars

Grazing on Melrose
Serves 6

Cream of Tomato and Carrot Soup With Fennel

Fresh Beet, Belgian Endive, and Gruyère Salad

Grilled Swordfish With Fresh Tomato-Mint Chutney

Wild Rice Pilaf in Pasilla Chiles

Chocolate-Raspberry Truffle Cheesecake

A Tasting of Assorted Zinfandels

Yunnan Tea

Melrose Avenue in Los Angeles is an exciting part of the city for strolling and looking. It has many trendy restaurants, interesting art galleries, antique shops, and stores selling vintage and funky clothing, art deco furnishings, and accessories. Several miles from beginning to end, this lively avenue must be explored in sections.

This is a grazing menu, inspired by some of the restaurants on Melrose Avenue. It reflects the culinary mix of ingredients and cuisines that typifies the fare you would find in this area. The emphasis is on fresh, flavorful, and not too heavy. It would make a perfect summer dinner, when tomatoes are at their seasonal best and when grills get the most use.

CREAM OF TOMATO AND CARROT SOUP WITH FENNEL

Fennel, an anise-flavored vegetable, is frequently used in Italian cooking. When raw, it has a pronounced flavor and a crunchy texture. When cooked, the flavor develops a more subtle sweetness. To cut the fennel bulb into strips, first trim away the feathery leaves and ribs. Halve the bulb, remove the core, and then slice each half lengthwise into thin strips.

- 1 medium onion, chopped
- 6 tablespoons unsalted butter
- 5 medium carrots, chopped
- 1 tart green apple, peeled, cored, and chopped
- 2 large cloves garlic, minced
- 2½ pounds tomatoes, peeled, seeded, and coarsely chopped
- 4 cups chicken stock, preferably homemade
- 1 tablespoon fresh lemon juice
- 1 teaspoon salt
- Bouquet garni (10 peppercorns, 2 bay leaves, and 1½ teaspoons fennel seed tied in a cheesecloth bag)
- 1 cup half-and-half
- Salt and freshly ground pepper, to taste
- 1 bulb fresh fennel, julienned, for garnish

1. In a large stockpot, sauté onion in 4 tablespoons of the butter, stirring occasionally, until translucent (about 6 minutes). Add carrots, apple, and garlic; sauté an additional 6 minutes.

2. Add tomatoes, stock, lemon juice, salt, and bouquet garni. Reduce heat, cover, and simmer until thickened (45 minutes).

3. Discard bouquet garni. Purée soup in small batches in a blender. Return to clean stockpot. Blend in half-and-half. Rewarm over low heat. Season with salt and pepper.

4. Sauté fennel in the remaining butter and use to garnish each serving of soup.

Serves 6 to 8

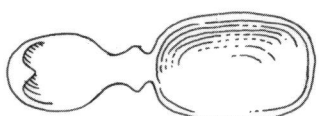

FRESH BEET, BELGIAN ENDIVE, AND GRUYÈRE SALAD

If your produce market is especially well stocked, it might carry the unusual golden baby beet. Its exotic color is particularly dramatic in this salad.

- 1 bunch golden baby beets
- 2 heads butter lettuce
- 2 heads Belgian endive
- ¾ cup diced Gruyère cheese
- ½ cup chopped toasted walnuts
- Orange-Walnut Vinaigrette (see below)

1. In a medium saucepan boil beets just until tender (about 20 minutes). Drain and let sit until cooled to room temperature (about 30 minutes). Peel and stem beets.

2. Arrange butter lettuce leaves on individual salad plates. Cut endive crosswise in ¼-inch circles and arrange on top of lettuce leaves. Divide whole cooked baby beets among salad plates.

3. Sprinkle with cheese and nuts. Spoon Orange-Walnut Vinaigrette over salad.

Serves 6 as part of a multicourse meal

Orange-Walnut Vinaigrette

- ¼ cup walnut oil
- ¼ cup vegetable oil
- ¼ cup fresh orange juice
- 2 tablespoons balsamic vinegar
- 2 teaspoons grated orange rind
- 1 to 2 teaspoons minced fresh tarragon or chervil

Combine all ingredients. Whisk to blend.

Makes about 1¼ cups

GRILLED SWORDFISH WITH FRESH TOMATO-MINT CHUTNEY

A chutney is usually a sweet fruit relish, but this version resembles another type of condiment, a salsa. Its mixture of fresh, stimulating tastes adds zest to the subtle flavor of the swordfish.

- ⅓ cup olive oil
- 2 tablespoons fresh lemon juice
- 6 swordfish steaks
- Salt and freshly ground pepper, to taste
- Fresh Tomato-Mint Chutney (see opposite page)

1. In a small bowl combine olive oil and lemon juice. Place swordfish steaks on a flat dish. Pour olive oil mixture over swordfish and marinate 1 hour.

2. Prepare a barbecue with hot coals (preferably mesquite). Grill swordfish 5 to 6 minutes on each side, basting with oil as needed. Season with salt and pepper. Serve with Fresh Tomato-Mint Chutney.

Serves 6

Fresh Tomato-Mint Chutney

- ⅓ cup minced fresh mint
- ¼ cup minced cilantro
- 1 teaspoon finely grated orange rind
- 3 tablespoons minced red onion
- ½ teaspoon salt
- 1 tablespoon tomato paste
- ⅓ cup fresh orange juice
- 2 tablespoons fresh lime juice
- 2 large tomatoes, cut in ½-inch dice
- 1 tablespoon minced jalapeño chile

In a medium glass bowl, combine mint, cilantro, orange rind, red onion, and salt. Stir with wooden spoon, bruising mint and cilantro to release oils. Add tomato paste, orange juice, and lime juice; mix well. Stir in tomatoes and chile.

Makes about 1¼ cups

• WILD RICE PILAF IN PASILLA CHILES •

Fresh *pasilla* chiles are usually available at specialty produce markets; Anaheim chiles can be substituted. Use caution when handling chiles; wear gloves and keep hands away from eyes.

- ⅓ cup small pieces dried vermicelli
- 4 tablespoons butter
- ⅓ cup finely chopped onion
- 1 cup wild rice
- 2 cups chicken stock
- Salt and freshly ground pepper, to taste
- ½ cup fresh or frozen corn kernels
- ½ cup toasted pecan pieces
- 6 pasilla chiles
- ½ cup grated Monterey jack cheese

1. In a large skillet cook vermicelli in butter over low heat, stirring, until pasta turns golden brown (5 to 6 minutes). Add onion and sauté 1 minute. Add wild rice and stir to coat with butter.

2. Stir in stock; season with salt and pepper. Cover and bring to a boil. Reduce heat and cook 30 to 40 minutes; when rice is almost cooked (test after 30 minutes), add corn kernels and cook 5 minutes. Stir in pecan pieces.

3. Cut off top third of each chile (discard or reserve for another use) and remove seeds. Place chiles on rack in steamer and cook 8 minutes.

4. Preheat oven to 350° F. Fill chiles with pilaf, set in baking dish, and bake 8 minutes; sprinkle with cheese and bake 2 minutes more.

Serves 6

CHOCOLATE-RASPBERRY TRUFFLE CHEESECAKE

The combination of chocolate and raspberry is irresistible. To toast the hazelnuts, spread them on a baking sheet and cook in a preheated 350° F oven for 5 to 7 minutes; let cool slightly. Place nuts in a cloth towel and rub to remove skins.

2½	cups finely crushed chocolate cookie crumbs	1½	pounds cream cheese, softened
½	cup toasted, skinned, and chopped hazelnuts	¼	cup plus 2 tablespoons sugar
		4	eggs
10	tablespoons butter, melted	3	tablespoons raspberry liqueur
1	package (12 oz) semisweet chocolate chips	1	cup sour cream
		½	cup fresh raspberries, for garnish
½	cup whipping cream		Raspberry Sauce (see page 45), for accompaniment (optional)
¾	cup seedless raspberry jam		

1. Preheat oven to 350° F. In a medium bowl combine crushed cookie crumbs and chopped hazelnuts. Stir in 6 tablespoons of the melted butter. Press mixture firmly onto the bottom and 2 inches up the sides of a 10-inch springform pan. Bake 6 minutes; cool.

2. In the top of a double boiler, combine chocolate chips and cream. Place over hot (not boiling) water and melt chocolate. Add raspberry jam and whisk until smooth; set aside.

3. In a food processor or with an electric mixer, blend cream cheese and the ¼ cup sugar. Add eggs, one at a time, and process until smooth. Blend in melted chocolate mixture, the remaining melted butter, and 2 tablespoons of the raspberry liqueur.

4. Pour into cooled crust. Bake until set (about 1 hour). Remove and cool 45 minutes.

5. If oven has been turned off, preheat to 350° F. Stir together sour cream, the remaining 2 tablespoons sugar, and the remaining 1 tablespoon raspberry liqueur. Spread over top of cheesecake. Bake 6 minutes. Cool, then cover and chill. Garnish with raspberries, and serve with Raspberry Sauce, if desired.

Serves 10 to 12

Variation

Cheesecake can also be baked in a 9- by 13-inch baking pan. For topping combine 2 cups sour cream, 2 tablespoons sugar, and 2 tablespoons raspberry liqueur. When cheesecake has chilled thoroughly, cut into 1-inch squares. Garnish each square with a fresh raspberry and serve in pastel paper cups.

Nibbling Around Nob Hill

Serves 6

Artichoke Dip With French Bread

A Plate of Three Little Salads:
Mushroom, Pea, and Wild Rice Salad;
Pear, Gorgonzola, and Toasted Pecan Salad;
Turkey, Jicama, and Bell Pepper Salad

Crab Cakes With Cilantro-Cayenne Mayonnaise

Spicy Vegetable Fritters With
Mustard Mayonnaise and Tuscan Garlic Sauce

Gingerbread

Lemon-Almond Chess Tart

A Tasting of Several Sauvignon Blancs

Gunpowder Tea (Dinner)

Earl Grey Tea (Dessert)

San Francisco is one of my favorite cities. I have fond memories of riding the ferries with my father as a child and of frequent trips north to "the City" from San Jose State University where I attended college. My husband's business activities have often taken us to the Bay Area, so I have had ample opportunity to enjoy its exciting cuisine.

This menu includes an appetizer artichoke dip from the White Swan and the Petite Auberge bed-and-breakfast inns on Nob Hill. The Lemon-Almond Chess Tart reminds me of the fine pastries at another Nob Hill hotel, the Stanford Court, where a lovely afternoon tea is served. The crab cakes and salads were inspired by Fog City Diner, an upscale, always crowded eating spot not on Nob Hill, but nearby. For this menu, serve all three salads on one plate as a single course; however, for other meals, each salad can be served on its own.

• ARTICHOKE DIP •

Keep this appetizer in mind the next time you are asked to bring something to a potluck party. It can be assembled in advance and baked when you arrive.

- 3 jars (6 oz each) artichoke hearts, drained and coarsely chopped
- ¾ cup mayonnaise
- ½ cup grated mozzarella cheese
- ¼ cup freshly grated Parmesan cheese
- Minced garlic, to taste
- 1 loaf French bread, sliced or cut into chunks, for accompaniment

Preheat oven to 350° F. Combine artichoke hearts, mayonnaise, mozzarella cheese, Parmesan cheese, and minced garlic. Place in a 1½-quart baking dish and bake 30 minutes. Serve with crusty French bread.

Makes 3 cups, serves 8

• MUSHROOM, PEA, AND WILD RICE SALAD •

Rice salads have always been popular. Wild rice has a nutty flavor and chewy texture that is very appealing. It requires a longer cooking time than does long-grain white rice.

- ½ pound domestic mushrooms, thinly sliced
- 3 tablespoons fresh lemon juice
- 2 packages (4 oz each) wild rice, cooked according to package directions
- 2 cups frozen petite peas, blanched in 2 cups boiling water
- ⅓ cup minced green onion
- Mustard-Herb Vinaigrette (see below)

Combine mushrooms and lemon juice in large bowl. Stir in rice, peas, and onion. Add dressing and mix thoroughly. Chill.

Serves 10

Mustard-Herb Vinaigrette

- 1 clove garlic, minced
- 2 teaspoons Dijon-style mustard
- 1 teaspoon salt
- ½ teaspoon freshly ground pepper
- 1 tablespoon minced fresh tarragon
- ¼ cup white wine vinegar
- ½ cup olive oil

Combine all ingredients and whisk.

Makes about ¾ cup

PEAR, GORGONZOLA, AND TOASTED PECAN SALAD

Fruit and cheese are a traditional combination. Gorgonzola is a rich, creamy blue-veined cheese that is also delicious as a garnish for a simple salad of tossed greens.

- 6 ripe pears, cored and cut in ¾-inch chunks
- 8 ounces Gorgonzola cheese, crumbled
- 1½ cups diced toasted pecans
- 1½ cups mayonnaise
- 4 tablespoons honey
- 4 tablespoons whipping cream
- 8 red leaf lettuce cups

In a mixing bowl combine pears, cheese, and toasted pecans. In a small bowl combine mayonnaise, honey, and whipping cream. Add to pears and stir gently. Divide salad among lettuce cups.

Serves 8

TURKEY, JICAMA, AND BELL PEPPER SALAD

Mushroom soy sauce is available at Asian markets. It is thicker and more flavorful than regular soy sauce. However, if necessary, you can use the regular type for the Jalapeño-Soy Dressing.

- 1 cup julienned jicama
- 1 red bell pepper, julienned
- 1 green bell pepper, julienned
- 1 yellow bell pepper, julienned
- ⅔ cup sliced green onion
- 3 cups julienned cooked turkey

Jalapeño-Soy Dressing (see below)
- 2 cups cilantro
- ½ cup fresh mint leaves
- 3½ cups mixed salad greens (butter lettuce, watercress, red leaf lettuce)

1. In a large bowl combine jicama, bell peppers, onion, and turkey. Add dressing. Mince ½ cup cilantro leaves and add to turkey mixture. Marinate several hours.

2. To serve, combine remaining cilantro and mint in a salad bowl with mixed greens. Add marinated turkey mixture and toss gently to combine.

Serves 8

Jalapeño-Soy Dressing

- 1 tablespoon minced jalapeño chile
- 1 large clove garlic, minced
- ⅔ cup safflower oil
- ¼ cup red wine vinegar
- 1 tablespoon mushroom soy sauce
- 2 tablespoons fresh lemon juice
- 2 teaspoons sugar
- 2 teaspoons sesame oil
- ¼ teaspoon salt

In a medium bowl combine jalapeño, garlic, oil, vinegar, soy sauce, lemon juice, sugar, sesame oil, and salt; set aside.

Makes about 1½ cups

CRAB CAKES WITH CILANTRO-CAYENNE MAYONNAISE

This recipe is my version of the popular, crispy crab cakes served at Fog City Diner. The spicy mayonnaise adds further heat to this dish.

- 2 eggs
- 6 tablespoons whipping cream
- 2 teaspoons dry mustard
- ½ teaspoon salt
- ½ teaspoon cayenne pepper
- 4 dashes hot-pepper sauce
- 4 tablespoons minced parsley
- 4 tablespoons minced white onion
- 2 pounds crabmeat, bone and cartilage removed, and flaked
- 3 tablespoons flour
- ½ cup butter
- Lemon wedges, for garnish
- Cilantro-Cayenne Mayonnaise (see below), for accompaniment

1. In a mixing bowl combine eggs, cream, mustard, salt, cayenne, pepper sauce, parsley, and onion. In another bowl combine crab with flour and add to egg mixture.

2. Form crab mixture into 24 round cakes.

3. In a large, heavy-bottomed skillet, heat butter and fry cakes until lightly browned on each side (about 5 minutes per side). Serve crab cakes with lemon wedges and Cilantro-Cayenne Mayonnaise.

Serves 6 to 8

Cilantro-Cayenne Mayonnaise

- 1 cup mayonnaise
- 2 tablespoons fresh lemon juice or sherry wine vinegar
- ⅛ to ¼ teaspoon cayenne pepper, to taste
- 2 tablespoons finely minced cilantro

Combine all ingredients.

Makes 2 cups

SPICY VEGETABLE FRITTERS

Chick-pea flour is available at Indian and some Middle Eastern markets. You may also want to try Creamy Mint Sauce (see page 68) for dipping.

- 1 cup sifted chick-pea flour
- 1 teaspoon vegetable oil
- ¼ teaspoon dry mustard
- ½ teaspoon salt
- ¼ teaspoon turmeric
- ¼ teaspoon ground cumin
- ¼ teaspoon ground coriander
- ¼ teaspoon cayenne pepper
- ½ teaspoon poppy seed
- ¼ teaspoon baking powder
- 1 teaspoon cornstarch
- ¾ cup (approximately) water
- Oil, for deep-frying
- 3 cups assorted vegetables (bell peppers, broccoli, squash, eggplant, green onion, thin slices of sweet potato), cut into bite-sized pieces
- Salt, for sprinkling
- Mustard Mayonnaise (see opposite page)
- Tuscan Garlic Sauce (see opposite page)

1. In a large mixing bowl, combine chick-pea flour, oil, mustard, salt, turmeric, cumin, coriander, cayenne, poppy seed, baking powder, and cornstarch.
2. Gradually mix in enough water to make a thick batter that will generously coat vegetables.
3. In a deep fryer heat oil to 350° F. Dip vegetables in batter to coat. Cook in small batches until golden (5 to 6 minutes). Drain on paper towels and sprinkle with salt. Serve with Mustard Mayonnaise and Tuscan Garlic Sauce.

Serves 4 as a first course, 6 as a side dish

Mustard Mayonnaise

½ cup mayonnaise   2 teaspoons Dijon-style mustard

In a small bowl combine mayonnaise and mustard; blend thoroughly.

Makes ½ cup

Tuscan Garlic Sauce

1 bulb garlic   ½ teaspoon white pepper
4 egg yolks   2 tablespoons hot water
1 teaspoon salt   1½ cups olive oil

In food processor purée peeled cloves from the bulb of garlic. Add egg yolks, salt, pepper, and the hot water; process 20 seconds. With machine on, slowly add olive oil. If mixture is too thick, add a little more hot water.

Makes 2 cups

• GINGERBREAD •

Homey American desserts like gingerbread, formerly considered too plain for restaurant fare, have become favorites of many of today's creative young chefs. This recipe would make a delicious trifle: Slice the gingerbread ½ inch thick; sprinkle the slices with orange-flavored liqueur and layer with *crème anglaise* (custard sauce) and prepared mincemeat.

1½ cups sifted flour   ½ cup margarine
½ teaspoon salt   ½ cup firmly packed brown sugar
½ teaspoon baking powder   ½ cup molasses
½ teaspoon baking soda   1 egg, beaten
1 teaspoon ground ginger   ½ cup buttermilk
1 teaspoon ground cinnamon   Whipped cream, for accompaniment

1. Preheat oven to 350° F. Grease an 8-inch square baking pan. In a large bowl sift flour with salt, baking powder, baking soda, ginger, and cinnamon. In another bowl cream margarine and sugar together until light and fluffy. Slowly add molasses and cream well (mixture may look curdled). Add egg and beat well.
2. Alternately add sifted dry ingredients and buttermilk to creamed margarine mixture, beginning and ending with dry ingredients.
3. Bake 35 minutes. Serve warm with whipped cream.

Serves 6 to 8

• LEMON-ALMOND CHESS TART •

Chess pies and tarts appear in many southern cookbooks. Some food historians say that *chess* evolved from *cheese*, perhaps a long-forgotten ingredient. Today the filling base is typically butter, eggs, and sugar. Richer versions include cream. Here the cream is omitted, but the filling is livened with lemon juice and almond. If you have a source of edible flowers, a garnish of scented geranium blossoms would be lovely.

The fresh, creative cuisine of San Francisco inspires a multicourse tea menu. In the foreground are Spicy Vegetable Fritters With Tuscan Garlic Sauce, Artichoke Dip With French Bread, and Crab Cakes With Cilantro-Cayenne Mayonnaise. In the large basket is a collection of three salads. The recipes begin on page 86.

Pâte Brisée (see below)
¾ cup butter, softened
1 cup sugar
4 teaspoons cornstarch
⅛ teaspoon salt
4 eggs, plus 2 egg yolks
¾ cup fresh lemon juice
2 tablespoons finely grated lemon rind
½ teaspoon almond extract
1 cup toasted sliced almonds
Confectioners' sugar, for dusting
Lemon slices, for garnish

1. Preheat oven to 400° F. Roll out Pâte Brisée and fit into a 10-inch tart pan with removable bottom. Prick pastry bottom with fork. Line pastry with parchment paper and fill with pie weights or dried beans.

2. Bake 10 minutes. Remove parchment paper and weights; set tart aside on a wire rack. Reduce oven temperature to 350° F.

3. With electric mixer cream butter until light and fluffy. Gradually add sugar and beat until light and fluffy. Blend in cornstarch and salt. Mix in eggs, one at a time, beating well after each addition; add egg yolks and beat some more. Mix in lemon juice, lemon rind, and almond extract.

4. Pour filling into crust; bake until top is pale golden brown and filling is set (about 30 minutes). Cool on a wire rack.

5. While tart is still warm, remove pan sides. Garnish around edge of tart top with sliced almonds, pressing them slightly into warm filling; cool completely.

6. To serve, dust with confectioners' sugar and arrange an overlapping ring of lemon slices in center of tart top.

Serves 8 to 10

Pâte Brisée

2 cups sifted flour, plus flour for kneading dough
1 teaspoon sugar
¾ teaspoon salt
½ cup unsalted butter, chilled and cut in 8 pieces
¼ cup vegetable shortening, well chilled and cut in small pieces
6 tablespoons chilled water
1 egg yolk

In a large bowl combine flour, sugar, and salt. With a pastry blender cut butter and shortening into flour until crumbly; do not overwork. Whisk water and egg yolk to blend. Add to dry ingredients and blend with a fork. Gather dough into a rough ball. On a lightly floured surface, knead dough into a smooth ball. Wrap in plastic and chill 30 minutes.

Makes one 10-inch tart shell

A Very British Farm Tea
Serves 6

Potted Shrimp With Water Biscuits

Watercress Sprigs With French Vinaigrette

Beef Steak and Kidney Pie

Colcannon

Port Onion Nibbles

Cold Baked Ham With Cranberry Chutney

Hearty Breads for Sandwiches

Spicy-Sweet Mustard Sauce

Dundee Cake

Keemun Tea

British high tea is a supper meal usually served at 6 p.m. It originated with farm workers and their families and included leftover cold roasted meats from the hearty dinner served at lunchtime. On blustery fall days and frequently throughout the cold winter, a hearty soup was also included.

When planning a tea, I like to prepare a baked ham for dinner one evening and then use the leftover meat for tea sandwiches and salads. For this menu that serves six people, you will need about 1½ pounds sliced baked ham for sandwiches. Dark and light rye, pumpernickel, onion, and whole-grain breads and rolls are good choices to accompany the ham.

The Port Onion Nibbles are a favorite I prepare during the holidays—they make an attractive garnish to arrange around a roast turkey that is brought to the table whole for carving.

POTTED SHRIMP WITH WATER BISCUITS

Potted Shrimp, a traditional British dish, may also be used as a filling for tea sandwiches or hollowed cherry tomatoes, or as a spread on thick cucumber slices.

- ½ pound cooked bay shrimp, chopped
- 3 ounces cream cheese, softened
- 2 tablespoons butter, softened
- 2 teaspoons fresh lemon juice
- 1 teaspoon prepared horseradish
- 4 or 5 drops hot-pepper sauce
- 1 tablespoon finely minced green onion
- 2 teaspoons minced dill
- Water biscuits, for accompaniment

Combine all ingredients and mix well. Refrigerate in covered container. Serve with water biscuits.

Makes 1¼ cups, serves 6 generously

WATERCRESS SPRIGS WITH FRENCH VINAIGRETTE

I once carried this vinaigrette with me on a backpacking trip because I had heard that we would find wild watercress near our camp. The greens were there as described and we enjoyed a delicious fresh salad after a strenuous 10-mile hike.

- 2 bunches watercress, washed and tough stems discarded
- ½ cup safflower oil
- 2 tablespoons olive oil
- 3 tablespoons fresh lemon juice
- 1 tablespoon grated onion
- ¾ teaspoon dry mustard
- ½ teaspoon Beau Monde seasoning or celery salt
- ¼ teaspoon white pepper
- 2 teaspoons fresh tarragon *or* ½ teaspoon crushed dried tarragon
- ½ teaspoon salt
- 1 clove garlic, finely minced
- 1 teaspoon sugar

Place watercress sprigs in serving bowl. Combine remaining ingredients, mix well, and add enough of this dressing to coat watercress. Leftover dressing may be reserved for future use; this dressing is also a good marinade for vegetables.

Serves 6

• BEEF STEAK AND KIDNEY PIE •

This is one of the best-known examples of British pub food. An ovenproof glazed pottery baking dish makes an attractive container for such substantial and hearty fare.

- ¼ teaspoon salt
- ¼ teaspoon freshly ground pepper
- ¼ teaspoon paprika
- ¼ cup flour
- ¾ pound top sirloin, cut in 1-inch cubes
- ½ pound beef or veal kidneys, trimmed of fat and membrane and cut in ⅛-inch slices
- 1 medium onion, peeled and thinly sliced
- ¼ cup butter
- 8 mushrooms, sliced
- 2 cups beef stock
- 1 bay leaf
- Single Crust Pastry (see page 26)
- 2 hard-cooked eggs, sliced

1. Combine salt, pepper, paprika, and flour; dredge beef cubes and kidney slices.

2. In a large skillet sauté onion in 2 tablespoons butter. Remove with slotted spoon to plate and set aside. Add remaining butter and sauté mushroom slices; remove with slotted spoon to another plate and set aside. In same pan brown dredged meat in hot fat, stirring occasionally. Add stock, bay leaf, and sautéed onion. Reduce heat, cover, and simmer until meat is tender (1 hour). Remove from heat and discard bay leaf; cool.

3. Preheat oven to 425° F. Roll out pastry dough to fit top of baking dish. Place beef mixture in 1½-quart baking dish; top with sliced eggs and sautéed mushrooms. Cover with pastry and seal sides. Cut vents for steam to escape.

4. Bake 10 to 15 minutes, then reduce heat to 350° F and bake until crust is golden brown (15 to 20 minutes).

Serves 6

• COLCANNON •

Colcannon is an Irish dish traditionally made from mashed potatoes, cabbage, and green onions. It is a fine accompaniment to roast beef or roast leg of lamb.

- 6 medium potatoes, peeled and quartered
- 4 cups finely shredded green cabbage
- ¼ cup butter
- ½ to ¾ cup lukewarm milk
- ½ cup finely sliced green onion (including some of the green tops)
- Salt and freshly ground pepper, to taste
- 1 tablespoon finely chopped parsley

1. In a large saucepan boil potatoes briskly until tender (35 to 40 minutes); drain.

2. In a separate saucepan cover cabbage with water and boil until tender (about 8 minutes). Drain thoroughly, squeezing out water. In a heavy skillet cook cabbage in 2 tablespoons butter 2 minutes, stirring constantly. Cover skillet and remove from heat.

3. Return potatoes to pan. Shake over low heat until dry. Add remaining butter and ½ cup milk. Mash potatoes; add additional milk as needed to make a purée thick enough to hold its shape. Stir in green onions and cabbage. Season with salt and pepper.

4. Place in a warmed casserole dish, sprinkle with parsley, and serve; or, hold in low oven until ready to serve.

Serves 6

• PORT ONION NIBBLES •

These fragrant onions are a piquant accompaniment for poultry, meat dishes, and savory pies. They will keep in the refrigerator up to one week.

1½ cups port	2 pounds small whole white onions
¾ cup red wine vinegar	(¾ to 1 inch diameter), peeled
½ cup firmly packed brown sugar	3 tablespoons vegetable oil
½ cup dried currants	Salt, to taste
⅛ teaspoon cayenne pepper	1 tablespoon finely chopped jalapeño chile (optional)

1. In a large saucepan combine port, vinegar, sugar, currants, and cayenne. Boil rapidly, uncovered, until reduced to 1¼ cups; set aside.

2. In a large skillet sauté a single layer of onions in oil over medium-high heat until lightly browned (about 7 minutes), shaking pan to turn onions. Remove onions with slotted spoon and place in wine sauce. Bring sauce to a boil, cover, reduce heat, and gently simmer 10 minutes (the onions should be slightly crisp); cool. Add salt and chile, if used. Serve at room temperature.

Makes about 3 cups

• CRANBERRY CHUTNEY •

This chutney is the perfect accompaniment to ham or to a holiday turkey. It is also delicious as a tea sandwich filling when blended with cream cheese. Stored tightly covered in the refrigerator, the chutney will keep up to 3 weeks. If processed in a hot water bath, it will keep up to one year. Pour chutney into sterilized jars, leaving about ¼ inch of headspace. Seal and process in a hot water bath 5 minutes.

4 cups (16 oz) fresh cranberries	½ teaspoon *each* ground cinnamon, allspice, ginger, and mace
1¾ cups water	1 teaspoon salt
1 cup red wine vinegar	⅛ to ¼ teaspoon cayenne pepper, to taste
3 cups firmly packed brown sugar	
Grated rind of 3 large oranges	3 large oranges, peeled, white membrane removed, sectioned, and coarsely chopped
¼ cup honey	
1 large onion, diced	
2 cups golden raisins	
2 large cloves garlic, minced	

1. In a 6-quart nonaluminum saucepan, combine fresh cranberries, the water, and vinegar. Bring to a boil over high heat; cook, uncovered, until cranberries pop (about 5 minutes).

2. Stir in sugar, orange rind, honey, onion, raisins, garlic, spices, salt, and cayenne. Return to a boil; reduce heat and simmer, uncovered, 1½ hours, stirring occasionally.

3. Stir in orange pulp; simmer until mixture thickens to consistency of jam (about 15 minutes).

Makes 5 pints

• SPICY-SWEET MUSTARD SAUCE •

Use this thick sauce as a spread for ham or other meat sandwiches (including hamburgers). Note that the sauce must stand for several hours before serving.

- ½ cup mustard
- ½ cup white wine vinegar
- ¼ cup sugar
- 2 egg yolks

In a small bowl combine mustard and vinegar. Cover and let stand for several hours. In a double boiler combine sugar and egg yolks; stir in mustard-vinegar mixture. Cook over hot water, stirring frequently, until sauce thickens. Place in glass container or serving dish and refrigerate until ready to use. Serve chilled or let sit on counter 30 minutes before serving to warm to room temperature.

Makes ¾ cup

• DUNDEE CAKE •

This fruitcake is a typical English "tinned" cake, which means that it stores well. Such a cake was often on hand in English homes, ready to offer to unexpected guests.

- 1 cup butter, plus butter for greasing
- 2¼ cups flour, plus flour for dusting
- ¼ cup dried currants
- ¼ cup raisins
- 1 cup boiling water
- 1 cup sugar
- 5 eggs, at room temperature
- ¼ cup finely chopped candied orange peel
- 15 candied red cherries, quartered
- ¼ teaspoon salt
- 1 cup (about 5 oz) finely ground almonds
- 1 tablespoon finely grated orange rind
- 1 tablespoon half-and-half
- ½ teaspoon baking powder
- 2 tablespoons orange-flavored liqueur or sherry, for soaking

1. Grease bottom and sides of a 9-inch springform pan with butter and line bottom with buttered parchment paper; flour paper and sides of pan. Set aside.

2. Place currants and raisins in a small bowl. Pour the boiling water over them and soak 10 minutes. Drain and pat dry with paper towels; set aside.

3. Preheat oven to 300° F. In a large mixing bowl, cream butter to soften; add sugar and beat until mixture is light and fluffy. Add eggs, one at a time, beating thoroughly after each addition.

4. Combine currants, raisins, peel, and cherries with ¼ cup of the flour; set aside.

5. Sift remaining 2 cups of the flour with salt. Gradually add to butter mixture, mixing until just incorporated. Stir in fruit mixture, almonds, and orange rind. Add half-and-half and baking powder. Mix thoroughly.

6. Turn batter into prepared pan. Smooth top with spatula. Bake until wooden pick inserted in center of cake comes out clean (about 1 hour and 20 minutes).

7. Cool on wire rack. Wrap cake in cheesecloth and soak with orange-flavored liqueur; store in a tin with a tight fitting lid. Cake will keep about 10 days.

Serves 8

A Collector's High Tea
Serves 12

Rhubarb Punch

Mini-Tortillas With Guacamole and Shrimp

Pear Picadillo in Filo Baskets

Jicama, Mandarin Orange, and Green Bean Salad

Salmon Fillets With Wild Rice Dressing

Sugar Snap Peas With Leeks

A Tasting of Several Chardonnays

Fresh Fruit in Chocolate Tulip Cookie Cups

Late-Harvest Riesling

Darjeeling Tea

An elegant high tea is a fine showcase for sharing with your friends the latest additions to a personal collection—be it a collection of paintings, photographs, folk art, or antique china teapots. As guests arrive, mingle, and view the display, pass the Rhubarb Punch. If weather permits, serve the meal buffet-style in the garden. Most of the food can easily be prepared ahead and assembled just prior to serving. Set off the courses with colorful table appointments and a dramatic flower arrangement. For the wines, consider a selection from favorite wineries that have commissioned artists to design their labels.

• RHUBARB PUNCH •

The addition of fresh rhubarb lends an unexpected tang to a citrus-flavored punch. Use only the stalks; the leaves can be toxic and should be discarded.

- 4 cups diced rhubarb stalks
- ½ cup water
- ½ cup sugar
- ¼ cup fresh orange juice
- 2 tablespoons fresh lemon juice
- 1 can (6 oz) pink lemonade concentrate, thawed
- 1 bottle (32 oz) lemon-lime soda
- 1 bottle (750 ml) dry Riesling or Gewürztraminer wine

1. In a nonreactive saucepan combine rhubarb, water, and sugar; cook over medium heat until rhubarb is tender (8 to 10 minutes). Set aside to cool.

2. Place rhubarb mixture in a blender or food processor and purée until smooth.

3. In a large bowl combine puréed rhubarb, orange juice, lemon juice, and lemonade concentrate. To serve, pour into punch bowl and add soda and wine; mix to blend.

Makes twenty-four 3-ounce servings

• MINI-TORTILLAS WITH GUACAMOLE AND SHRIMP •

For this zesty hors d'oeuvre, use a biscuit cutter to form tiny tortillas. The rounds are then fried and topped with an easy-to-prepare guacamole and tiny shrimp.

- 2 ripe avocados
- ¼ cup prepared salsa
- 2 tablespoons fresh lemon juice
- ½ cup sour cream
- Salt and freshly ground pepper, to taste
- 12 corn tortillas
- Oil, for frying
- ½ pound cooked baby shrimp
- Cilantro leaves, for garnish

1. For the guacamole, halve avocados, remove pit, scoop out pulp, and mash slightly with a fork (pulp will still be chunky). Combine with salsa, lemon juice, and sour cream; mix until smooth. Season with salt and pepper. Set aside.

2. With a 2-inch round biscuit cutter, cut small circles from tortillas. In a large skillet heat oil; fry tortilla rounds until puffed. Drain well on paper towels.

3. To serve, spoon a small amount of guacamole on each round. Top with shrimp and a few cilantro leaves.

Makes about 48 mini-tortillas

• PEAR PICADILLO IN FILO BASKETS •

The Pear Picadillo has an unusual and appealing sweet-spicy flavor. It can also be used in a southwestern menu (see page 75) as an appetizer. The Filo Baskets are versatile too; filled with Lemon Curd (see page 78) or Orange Curd (see page 79), they make an elegant dessert. The baskets can be prepared ahead and frozen in the muffin tins for several weeks. Reheat in a 350° F oven for 5 minutes before filling.

1 tomato, peeled and cored	¼ teaspoon sugar
1 firm, ripe pear, peeled and cored	¼ teaspoon ground cinnamon
2 whole canned green chiles	⅛ teaspoon ground cloves
1 tablespoon vegetable oil	⅛ teaspoon cayenne pepper
1 onion, chopped	1 tablespoon red wine vinegar
1 clove garlic, minced	⅓ cup raisins
1 pound lean ground chuck	Filo Baskets (see below)
1¼ teaspoons chili powder	Sour cream, for garnish
1 teaspoon salt	⅓ cup pine nuts, for garnish
½ teaspoon ground cumin	2 tablespoons chopped fresh
½ teaspoon dried oregano leaves, crushed	jalapeño chile, for garnish

1. In a food processor fitted with metal blade, chop tomato, pear, and green chiles.

2. In a large skillet, heat oil and sauté onion over medium heat 3 minutes; add garlic and sauté 1 minute more. Remove with slotted spoon and set aside.

3. In same pan cook meat until it loses its red color (about 6 minutes). Add reserved onion and garlic, and chili powder, salt, cumin, oregano, sugar, cinnamon, cloves, cayenne pepper, vinegar, raisins, and tomato-pear mixture. Stir to combine and simmer over low heat about 20 minutes.

4. Preheat oven to 350° F. Divide filling among Filo Baskets. Carefully set filled baskets on a baking sheet and heat 5 minutes. To serve, garnish each filled basket with sour cream, pine nuts, and chile.

Serves 12

Filo Baskets

12 sheets filo dough, thawed according to package directions	⅓ cup finely ground dried bread crumbs
1½ cups unsalted butter, melted	

Preheat oven to 350° F. Place 1 sheet filo dough on work surface. Brush with some melted butter and sprinkle with some bread crumbs. Butter 3 more sheets of dough, and sprinkle 2 of the 3 sheets with bread crumbs. Stack the dough, ending with sheet that is buttered but without crumbs. Repeat with remaining dough; you will have three stacks of filo dough, 4 sheets per stack. With kitchen scissors or a pizza cutter, cut each stack into twenty 3-inch squares. Brush miniature muffin cups with remaining butter. Press one square of stacked filo into each muffin cup, forming a basket. Bake until lightly browned (8 to 10 minutes). Cool in pan 5 minutes; remove and transfer to wire rack to cool completely.

Makes 60 filo baskets

JICAMA, MANDARIN ORANGE AND GREEN BEAN SALAD

This refreshing and colorful salad would also complement a menu featuring foods of Mexico. Jicama, a tuber, has a crisp texture and sweet taste. During the fall, garnish the salad with ruby-colored pomegranate seeds.

- 2 cups green beans, sliced diagonally
- 1 large jicama, peeled and julienned (about 2 cups)
- 3 cans (8 oz each) mandarin orange sections, drained
- Minted Orange-Walnut Vinaigrette (see below)
- 12 leaves red leaf lettuce

1. In a medium saucepan cook green beans in boiling, salted water over medium-high heat until tender-crisp (6 to 8 minutes). Drain and set aside to cool.

2. In a large bowl combine green beans, jicama, and orange sections. Pour dressing over salad mixture and gently stir to coat. Let marinate in refrigerator 30 minutes.

3. Arrange lettuce leaves on an attractive serving platter. With a slotted spoon, set an equal amount of vegetable mixture onto each lettuce leaf.

Serves 12

Minted Orange-Walnut Vinaigrette

- 2 tablespoons frozen orange juice concentrate, thawed
- ⅓ cup white wine vinegar or pineapple vinegar
- ⅔ cup walnut oil or ⅓ cup *each* walnut oil and vegetable oil
- ⅓ cup fresh mint leaves, minced
- 1 jalapeño chile, finely minced

In a medium bowl combine all ingredients.

Makes about 1½ cups

SALMON FILLETS WITH WILD RICE DRESSING

A gift of a whole salmon caught by a friend in Alaska was the inspiration for this recipe. I have served it with great success at a gathering of special friends for midnight supper on New Year's Eve. The entire recipe can be prepared the day before serving, refrigerated, and then baked when needed.

- 1 package (4 oz) wild rice
- 2 cups chicken broth
- 3 tablespoons unsalted butter, plus butter for greasing
- 2 fillets from a whole salmon (about 4 lb)
- 3 shallots, minced
- ¾ pound mushrooms, finely chopped
- 2 cups spinach leaves, washed, drained, and chopped
- 2 teaspoons minced fresh tarragon, or more, to taste
- ¼ to ½ teaspoon mace
- Salt and freshly ground pepper, to taste
- Fresh tarragon sprigs, for garnish
- Chardonnay Tarragon Sauce (see opposite page)

1. Cook wild rice according to package directions, using the chicken broth rather than water; set aside. Cut a piece of parchment paper the length and width of a baking dish (or a rimmed baking sheet) large enough to hold both salmon fillets. Grease one side of paper with butter and set in dish, buttered side up. Place salmon fillets on buttered paper. Set aside.

2. Preheat oven to 350° F. In a large skillet sauté shallots in the 3 tablespoons butter until translucent (2 to 3 minutes). Add mushrooms and cook until mixture thickens and mushroom liquid has cooked away (10 to 15 minutes). Add spinach and sauté until tender (about 3 minutes). Blend in wild rice, minced tarragon, and mace; season with salt and pepper.

3. Spread rice mixture evenly over surface of both fillets. Cover with aluminum foil; bake until knife inserted into the thickest part of fillet reveals that flesh is flaky (about 20 minutes).

4. To serve, arrange fillets on an attractive serving platter; cut each fillet in half lengthwise and then crosswise in 1½-inch strips. Garnish with tarragon sprigs and serve with Chardonnay Tarragon Sauce.

Serves 12

Chardonnay Tarragon Sauce

- 4 medium shallots, minced
- 1 cup Chardonnay wine
- 2 cups chicken stock (preferably homemade)
- 1½ cups whipping cream
- 2 to 3 tablespoons Creole or grainy mustard
- 1 to 2 tablespoons chopped fresh tarragon
- Salt and white pepper, to taste

In a medium saucepan combine shallots, wine, and stock. Cook over medium-high heat until reduced to 1 cup (25 to 30 minutes). Strain through a sieve, pressing shallots to extract juices. Return to saucepan and whisk in cream and mustard. Cook, stirring occasionally, over medium heat until thickened (15 to 20 minutes). Remove from heat, whisk in tarragon, and season with salt and pepper.

Makes 1½ cups

• SUGAR SNAP PEAS WITH LEEKS •

This dish was inspired by a meal I enjoyed at the French Laundry, a small restaurant in the heart of California's Napa Valley wine region. Sugar snap peas should be cooked just until tender in order to preserve their natural snap and bright green color.

- 3 pounds sugar snap peas
- 6 tablespoons butter
- 3 leeks (white part only), washed thoroughly and julienned
- 2 tablespoons minced fresh herbs (tarragon, chervil, or marjoram)
- Salt and freshly ground pepper, to taste

1. Blanch sugar snap peas in boiling water just until tender (about 5 minutes); drain, refresh in cold water, and set aside.

2. In a large skillet, melt butter and sauté leeks until tender (about 5 minutes). Add blanched sugar snap peas and sauté until heated through (about 3 minutes); stir in fresh herbs. Season with salt and pepper and serve warm.

Serves 12

FRESH FRUIT IN CHOCOLATE TULIP COOKIE CUPS

The cookie cups can be made early in the day, covered with waxed paper, and kept at room temperature until needed. Coat the cups with melted chocolate no more than 2 hours before serving so that the cookies don't get soggy.

Chocolate Tulip Cookie Cups (see below)
6 ripe peaches, peeled, seeded, and sliced
1 cup strawberries, stemmed and halved
1 cup blueberries
1 cup raspberries
1 cup whipping cream
2 tablespoons sugar
2 tablespoons orange-flavored liqueur

Arrange Chocolate Tulip Cookie Cups on attractive dessert plates. In a large bowl toss fruit gently to combine. In a separate bowl, whip cream until stiff peaks form; add sugar and liqueur during last minute or so of beating. Spoon fruit into cookie cups and pipe whipped cream rosettes on top of fruit.

Serves 12

Chocolate Tulip Cookie Cups

Solid vegetable shortening, for greasing
Flour, for dusting
5½ tablespoons unsalted butter, softened
½ cup sugar
¼ teaspoon salt
2 teaspoons orange-flavored liqueur
1 teaspoon finely grated orange rind
3 egg whites, at room temperature
½ cup plus 3 tablespoons flour
¾ teaspoon cornstarch
4 ounces semisweet chocolate, melted

1. Preheat oven to 375° F. Grease 2 baking sheets with solid vegetable shortening and dust with flour; shake off excess flour. Draw 2 circles (6 to 7 inches across) on each of the baking sheets.

2. In a medium bowl with electric mixer, cream butter until fluffy. Gradually beat in sugar; add salt, liqueur, and orange rind and mix thoroughly. Slowly beat in egg whites. Fold in flour and cornstarch until batter is smooth.

3. In center of each circle on baking sheet, place 1 tablespoon batter and spread with a spatula to fill circle (the batter will be very thin). Bake 5 minutes, then start checking cookies (remove when just slightly browned). Remove each cookie with a long metal spatula and invert over a glass custard cup. Top cookie with another custard cup and press cookie into a flower shape. After 30 seconds remove top custard cup and set cookie cup upside down on cooling rack.

4. Repeat with remainder of batter. Cool completely and then gently lift cookies off of custard cups. Using a pastry brush, paint bottom and partway up sides of cookie cups with melted chocolate. Set, right side up, on wire racks, until chocolate sets (about 30 minutes).

Makes 12 to 14 cookie cups

TEA AT THREE
Serves 8

Herbed Coeur à la Crème

Assorted Tea Sandwiches (see page 18)

Ham, Cabbage, Gruyère, and Apple Salad

Lamb Vegetable Pasties

Dessert of the Season
Summer: Fresh Peach Trifle
Fall: Chocolate Marmalade Cake
Winter: Cranberry Pudding With Bourbon Custard Sauce
Spring: Chocolate-Dipped Strawberries

Earl Grey Tea

For this traditional afternoon tea meal I have offered a choice of four desserts, each matched both in ingredients and in mood to a particular time of year. The Fresh Peach Trifle is my interpretation of the well-known custard-and-cake confection, a recipe that is quintessentially English. The Chocolate Marmalade Cake is a rich temptation, flavored with a favorite preserve. Cranberry Pudding is a perfect holiday sweet, with a bourbon-spiked sauce. Chocolate-Dipped Strawberries takes the fresh, sweet flavor of berries just a step further with the complementary smoothness of the chocolate coating. The rest of the menu features an eclectic, international combination of dishes: British tea sandwiches and pasties, a French savory molded cheese, and a salad that is contemporary American.

• HERBED COEUR À LA CRÈME •

The French word for heart, *coeur*, describes dishes prepared in a heart shape, such as this molded savory cheese spread. More commonly, coeur à la crème is a sweet cheese dessert, such as the version that appears in the Valentine's Day Tea (see page 45). You will enjoy the contrast between the two dishes. Note that this dish needs to be refrigerated for 24 hours.

- 1 pint (16 oz) cottage cheese
- 4 ounces cream cheese, softened
- 1 tablespoon prepared horseradish
- 2 tablespoons minced fresh dill
- 2 tablespoons minced parsley
- 1 tablespoon minced fresh chervil or oregano
- 1 tablespoon minced fresh rosemary
- 2 tablespoons minced green onion
- Pinch of salt and white pepper
- 1 cup whipping cream
- 3 egg whites
- Cucumber rounds or crackers, for accompaniment

1. Line 1 large heart mold with cheesecloth that has been carefully rinsed. Set aside.

2. In a large bowl thoroughly combine cottage cheese and cream cheese. Add horseradish, dill, parsley, chervil, rosemary, green onion, and salt and pepper. Mix well.

3. In a medium bowl, whip the cream until soft peaks form; fold into cheese mixture. In another bowl whip egg whites until stiff but not dry and fold into cheese mixture.

4. Fill lined heart mold with cheese mixture, mounding it slightly. Bring hanging edges of cheesecloth over the top. Place mold on a rack over a shallow pan. Refrigerate at least 24 hours. The whey will drain out.

5. Unmold and serve with cucumber slices or crackers.

Serves up to 12, with other dishes

• HAM, CABBAGE, GRUYÈRE AND APPLE SALAD •

The sweet tartness of apple contrasts well with the smokiness of the cheese and ham in this colorful, crunchy salad. This dish is a good way to use leftover ham.

- 1 cup finely diced red cabbage
- ¾ cup diced Gruyère cheese
- 1 cup finely chopped cooked ham
- 2 apples, peeled, cored, and chopped fine
- ¾ cup mayonnaise
- 3 tablespoons fresh orange juice
- 2 teaspoons grated orange rind
- 6 radicchio or red cabbage leaves
- ½ cup finely chopped toasted pecans

In a large bowl combine cabbage, cheese, ham, and apples. In a small bowl mix mayonnaise, orange juice, and orange rind until smooth. Combine with cabbage mixture. Divide salad evenly among radicchio leaves; garnish with toasted pecans.

Serves 6 to 8

Photograph, Page 106: Pick a dessert to match the season for this afternoon tea meal. In the summer serve Fresh Peach Trifle. In the fall choose Chocolate Marmalade Cake. During the winter months offer Cranberry Pudding With Bourbon Custard Sauce. For the spring consider Chocolate-Dipped Strawberries. Recipes for Tea at Three begin on page 103.

• LAMB VEGETABLE PASTIES •

Cornish miners carried meat-filled, half-moon-shaped pasties in their lunch pails each day. This version makes small pasties, suitable for tea fare. The filling is more exotic than what the miners enjoyed, with overtones of Middle Eastern cooking from the blend of cumin and cinnamon used as seasoning. The filling will keep for up to three days in the refrigerator.

2 tablespoons vegetable oil	½ teaspoon freshly ground pepper
1 pound trimmed leg of lamb, cut into ½-inch cubes	2 teaspoons ground cumin
	1 teaspoon ground cinnamon
1 large onion, finely diced	½ cup beef stock, plus additional stock if needed
½ cup fresh peas or thawed frozen peas	½ cup raisins
1 large carrot, chopped fine	Double recipe Double Crust Pastry (see page 120)
2 potatoes	
1 teaspoon salt	3 to 4 tablespoons milk or water

1. In a large, heavy-bottomed skillet, heat oil and sauté lamb cubes until browned (about 6 minutes). Add onion and sauté until limp (about 3 minutes).

2. In a small saucepan cook peas and carrots in a small amount of boiling water until tender (about 5 minutes); drain and add to meat mixture.

3. In same small saucepan, parboil potatoes 5 minutes; drain, peel, and grate. Add potato, salt, pepper, cumin, cinnamon, and stock to meat mixture; cook 5 minutes over medium heat (mixture should still be moist; if not, add additional beef stock). Stir in raisins; let cool slightly.

4. Preheat oven to 400° F. On a lightly floured work surface, roll out pastry ⅛ inch thick; with a 4-inch round biscuit cutter, cut out circles of dough. Place 2 tablespoons filling on each pastry circle. Moisten edge of circle with milk or water; fold dough in half, crimping edges with a fork to seal.

5. Arrange pasties on a parchment-lined baking sheet and bake until brown (15 to 20 minutes).

Makes 24 pasties

• FRESH PEACH TRIFLE •

Trifles are a wonderful choice for entertaining because they should be made at least a day ahead of serving to allow the flavors to mix and mellow. Buy the ladyfingers from a high-quality French bakery if you prefer not to make your own (see page 55).

- 20 to 24 ladyfingers
- ⅔ cup plus 2 tablespoons peach schnapps
- Peach Crème Anglaise (see below)
- 5 peaches, peeled and sliced
- Lemon Pound Cake, sliced (see below)
- 1 cup whipping cream
- 2 tablespoons sugar
- 1 pint raspberries, for garnish

1. Brush flat side of ladyfingers with ⅓ cup schnapps and arrange on sides and bottom of an attractive 6-cup glass serving dish.

2. Spoon half of Peach Crème Anglaise over ladyfingers lining bottom of dish. Place half of peach slices on top of crème anglaise. Brush cake slices on both sides with ⅓ cup schnapps. Place half of cake slices on top of peaches. Repeat layering with remaining crème anglaise, peaches, and cake slices.

3. In a medium bowl whip cream until medium-soft peaks form. Add sugar and the 2 tablespoons schnapps and continue beating until blended. Spread over top of trifle. Garnish with raspberries. Refrigerate until serving time.

Serves 8

Peach Crème Anglaise

- 8 egg yolks
- 6 tablespoons sugar
- 2¼ cups half-and-half
- 4 teaspoons cornstarch
- 3 tablespoons peach schnapps

1. In a medium bowl beat yolks until thickened. Gradually add sugar; beat until mixture is thick and lemon-colored. Transfer to a saucepan and whisk in 2 cups half-and-half. Mix cornstarch with remaining half-and-half and whisk into egg mixture.

2. Cook over medium-low heat, stirring constantly, until mixture thickens (6 to 8 minutes). Remove from heat and stir in schnapps. Cool and chill.

Makes about 3 cups

Lemon Pound Cake

- ¾ cup butter, plus butter for greasing
- 1¼ cups sifted flour, plus flour for dusting
- ½ teaspoon grated lemon rind
- ¾ cup sugar
- 3 eggs, at room temperature
- 1 teaspoon vanilla extract
- ½ teaspoon baking powder
- ¼ teaspoon salt

1. Preheat oven to 350° F. Butter and flour bottom of a 9- by 5-inch loaf pan. In a medium bowl cream the ¾ cup butter with lemon rind; gradually add sugar, beating until light and fluffy. Add eggs, one at a time, beating well after each addition; add vanilla.

2. Sift together 1¼ cups flour, baking powder, and salt; mix into creamed mixture.

3. Pour batter into prepared pan. Bake until done (about 50 minutes). Cool in pan 15 minutes, then remove and finish cooling on a wire rack.

Serves 8

• CHOCOLATE MARMALADE CAKE •

The glaze—infused with orange—helps this dense, moist cake keep well. An orange flavor also permeates the chocolate cake because of the orange marmalade in the batter.

- ¾ cup unsalted butter, softened, plus butter for greasing
- 1½ cups flour, plus flour for dusting
- 4 ounces semisweet chocolate
- 2 ounces unsweetened chocolate
- 1 teaspoon baking powder
- ⅛ teaspoon salt
- ⅔ cup sugar
- 5 eggs separated, at room temperature
- ½ teaspoon vanilla extract
- ¼ cup marmalade (preferably imported bitter style)
- ¼ cup ground blanched almonds
- Marmalade Glaze (see below)

1. Grease a 9-inch springform pan with butter and line bottom with buttered parchment paper. Flour paper and sides of pan; set aside.

2. Melt chocolates together in a double boiler over hot, not simmering water, stirring until chocolate melts. Remove from heat and let cool to room temperature.

3. Preheat oven to 350° F. Sift the 1½ cups flour, baking powder, and salt together. In a separate bowl, cream the ¾ cup butter until light; add sugar gradually, beating until mixture is light and fluffy. Add egg yolks, one at a time, beating thoroughly after each addition. Stir cooled chocolate, vanilla, and marmalade into butter mixture. Gradually mix in flour mixture until thoroughly combined. Stir in almonds. Batter will be stiff.

4. Beat egg whites until stiff peaks form. Fold one third of beaten whites into batter to lighten it. Carefully fold in remaining whites, in two stages.

5. Turn batter into prepared pan. Bake until wooden pick inserted in center of cake comes out clean (50 to 60 minutes). Cool cake in pan 5 minutes. Turn out onto wire rack and cool completely.

6. Poke holes in top of cake with a toothpick. Brush cake with warm Marmalade Glaze. Allow to set about 20 minutes before serving.

Serves 10 to 12

Marmalade Glaze

- ¼ cup marmalade, melted
- 2 tablespoons orange-flavored liqueur

In a small saucepan, melt marmalade; blend in liqueur.

Makes ¼ cup

CRANBERRY PUDDING WITH BOURBON CUSTARD SAUCE

Although baked rather than steamed, this dessert has the texture of a traditional steamed pudding. The cranberries, a seasonal touch, make it nicely tart. This pudding is a wonderful finish to a holiday dinner.

- 4 tablespoons unsalted butter, melted, plus butter for greasing
- 1 cup firmly packed brown sugar
- ½ cup plus 1 tablespoon whipping cream
- 2 large eggs, separated
- 2 teaspoons vanilla extract
- 1½ cups flour
- 1 teaspoon baking powder
- ½ teaspoon cream of tartar
- 1 teaspoon ground cinnamon
- ¼ teaspoon mace
- ⅛ teaspoon salt
- 3 cups coarsely chopped cranberries
- Grated rind of 1 orange
- ¾ cup chopped pecans
- Bourbon Custard Sauce (see below)

1. Preheat oven to 350° F. Butter an 8-inch square baking pan. In a small bowl combine brown sugar, cream, egg yolks, and vanilla and mix until well blended.

2. Sift together flour, baking powder, ¼ teaspoon cream of tartar, cinnamon, mace, and salt. Place dry ingredients in large bowl; mix in cranberries, orange rind, and nuts. Add brown sugar mixture and the 4 tablespoons melted butter and mix thoroughly.

3. In a separate bowl beat egg whites until foamy. Add ¼ teaspoon cream of tartar and beat until soft peaks form. Fold into batter.

4. Pour into prepared pan and bake until pudding is set (30 to 35 minutes). Serve with Bourbon Custard Sauce.

Serves 8 to 10

Bourbon Custard Sauce

- 5 egg yolks
- ⅓ cup sugar
- 1 cup milk
- ¾ cup whipping cream
- ½ teaspoon vanilla extract
- ¼ cup bourbon

1. In a medium bowl beat egg yolks and sugar together until thick. In a medium saucepan heat milk and cream over medium heat until almost boiling. Slowly add to egg yolk mixture, whisking constantly.

2. Return mixture to saucepan. Cook over low heat until thick and mixture coats the back of a metal spoon (about 6 minutes). Do not boil.

3. Strain into a bowl and whisk in vanilla and bourbon. Serve warm or chilled.

Makes about 2 cups

• CHOCOLATE-DIPPED STRAWBERRIES •

I have made hundreds of these extremely popular sweets at a time for large parties. The long-stemmed berries look very elegant and the combination of strawberry and chocolate is always irresistible to guests. A variation using white chocolate is also offered. Be sure to use the best chocolate—white or dark—that you can find. Coating chocolate is available at specialty food stores.

- 12 plump strawberries, stems attached
- ½ pound finest-quality semisweet or bittersweet coating chocolate
- 1 tablespoon solid vegetable shortening

1. Wash the strawberries and pat dry with paper towels. In a double boiler over hot but not boiling water, melt chocolate and vegetable shortening, stirring carefully. Leave bottom of double boiler over low flame and set top section with chocolate on a work surface (if chocolate begins to harden, return top of pan to heat to melt chocolate).

2. Stick a toothpick or skewer into stem end of each strawberry. Dip each berry into the chocolate, coating two thirds of the berry. Let the excess drip back into the pan. Stick toothpick ends into a Styrofoam block covered with plastic wrap.

3. Chill berries until chocolate sets (about 30 minutes). Chocolate-dipped berries will keep a day in the refrigerator. Remove toothpicks.

Makes 12 dipped strawberries

Variation

Substitute 6 ounces finest-quality white chocolate for the semisweet or bittersweet chocolate. Do not use vegetable shortening. Melt white chocolate in a double boiler over hot but not boiling water. Do not stir. White chocolate melts very slowly. Continue with steps 2 and 3 of Chocolate-Dipped Strawberries.

Teddy Bear Tea

Serves 6 to 8

Apricot Nectar
Celery Stuffed With Pimiento-Olive Cream Cheese
Waldorf Salad Supreme
Ham and Cheese Roll-Ups
Banana Spears Dipped in Chocolate, Coconut, and Peanuts
Teddy Bear Gingies
Hot Chocolate
Cinnamon Tea

In Carmel, California, one of the social events of the Christmas season is the annual Teddy Bear Tea. Guests are invited to dress their bears and bring them to the Willow Tearoom. Prizes are awarded in the following categories: Most Victorian or Edwardian, Most Sophisticated, Most Appropriate for the Holiday Season, and Most Handsome or Winsome Bare Bear.

This menu features foods dear to the hearts of children. Finger foods are always a favorite with the little ones. They love the chocolate-dipped bananas, which can be made early in the day. Cover the entire banana with chocolate.

Photograph, page 114: What else but Teddy Bear Gingies would be served at a holiday tea in honor of some favorite furry friends? Gingerbread cookies such as these are easy for children to prepare and decorate. The recipe is on page 117.

CELERY STUFFED WITH PIMIENTO-OLIVE CREAM CHEESE

The familiar cream cheese and olive sandwich is repackaged. Children love the crunch of celery and the smoothness of the creamy filling.

- 1 package (8 oz) cream cheese, softened
- ¼ cup finely chopped pitted black or green olives
- 2 tablespoons finely chopped canned pimientos
- 24 stalks celery

Combine cream cheese with chopped olive and pimiento and blend until smooth. Spread in celery stalks.

Makes 24 stuffed spears

WALDORF SALAD SUPREME

The classic apple-nut salad is updated with the addition of pears and Swiss cheese. Don't peel the apples; the bright red skin adds color to the salad.

- 2 Red Delicious apples, cored and diced
- 1 pear, cored and diced
- 2 tablespoons fresh lemon juice
- ¾ cup diced Swiss cheese
- ½ cup diced celery
- ½ cup chopped cashews
- ⅔ cup mayonnaise
- Lettuce leaves, for garnish

1. In a large bowl combine apples, pear, and lemon juice. Stir in Swiss cheese, celery, and cashews, then mayonnaise.
2. Chill and serve on lettuce leaves.

Serves 6 to 8

HAM AND CHEESE ROLL-UPS

Children will enjoy the crunch of pickle that they get with each bite of these layered rolls. Use sweet pickles if you think your guests might appreciate their flavor more. For adults try pickled baby corn.

- 16 ounces thinly sliced squares of boiled ham
- ½ cup mayonnaise mixed with 2 teaspoons mustard
- 8 ounces Monterey jack or American cheese, cut in matchstick pieces about ⅜ inch thick
- 1 dill pickle, cut in matchsticks

Spread ham slices with a thin layer of mayonnaise mixture. Place a piece of cheese and a piece of pickle at one end of each ham slice and roll into a cylinder.

Makes 18 to 20 roll-ups

Teatime Celebrations

BANANA SPEARS DIPPED IN CHOCOLATE, COCONUT, AND PEANUTS

Be sure to completely coat each piece of banana with chocolate; otherwise the fruit will darken when exposed to the air. If you find that you will often be making this or any recipe that calls for fruit to be dipped in chocolate, you may want to buy a special dipping fork, available at baking supply stores. The fork has two or three prongs or a loop; both models are designed to hold the fruit securely as it is lowered into the coating.

- ½ cup flaked coconut
- ½ cup chopped roasted, salted peanuts
- 12 ounces semisweet chocolate chips
- 1 tablespoon vegetable shortening
- 3 large bananas

1. Combine coconut and peanuts; set aside.

2. In a double boiler over hot (not boiling) water, melt chocolate and vegetable shortening together, stirring gently.

3. Peel bananas and slice each in half lengthwise; then cut each half into 3 pieces (making a total of 6 pieces per banana). Insert a toothpick in each piece of banana. Dip into melted chocolate, coating each piece well; let excess chocolate drip back into pan.

4. Dip each chocolate-covered banana into coconut-peanut mixture to coat. To avoid having to set down banana, stick end of toothpick into a Styrofoam block covered with plastic wrap. Chill until chocolate sets (about 30 minutes). Remove toothpicks and serve. The coated bananas can be made up to 1 day ahead and held in the refrigerator.

Makes 18 pieces

• TEDDY BEAR GINGIES •

I have always enjoyed baking holiday cookies, especially with the help of little hands. I usually prepare the dough a day ahead since it needs to chill. Frostings are made while the cookies are in the oven; it's always a contest to see who can do the most decorating while nibbling on frosting and candy sprinkles.

½ cup firmly packed brown sugar	1 teaspoon ground ginger
½ cup butter or margarine	½ teaspoon baking soda
½ cup molasses	¼ teaspoon salt
3 cups flour	1 egg, beaten
½ teaspoon ground cloves	Colored sprinkles, for decoration
½ teaspoon ground allspice	Confectioners' Sugar Frosting
1 teaspoon ground cinnamon	(see below)

1. In small saucepan combine sugar, butter, and molasses; heat to boiling, stirring constantly. Remove from heat. Pour into large mixing bowl and allow to cool.

2. Sift together flour, cloves, allspice, cinnamon, ginger, baking soda, and salt. Add egg to molasses mixture and mix slowly until well blended. Gradually add flour mixture until dough stiffens. Form a ball of dough and flatten slightly. Wrap in waxed paper or plastic wrap and refrigerate several hours or overnight.

3. Preheat oven to 350° F. Work with one third of dough at a time. On floured surface, roll out chilled dough ¼ inch thick. Using a floured 4-inch (or 2-inch) teddy bear cookie cutter, cut gingies. Carefully transfer to lightly greased baking sheets. Move arms and feet in different directions to create dancing bears.

4. Bake cookies until set and dry around edges (12 to 15 minutes for large cookies, about 9 minutes for small cookies). Carefully remove to wire racks and cool. Decorate with sprinkles and frosting as desired. Repeat with remaining dough.

Makes 2 dozen 4-inch cookies, 3 dozen 2-inch cookies

Confectioners' Sugar Frosting

2 cups confectioners' sugar	2 or 3 tablespoons half-and-half
¼ teaspoon vanilla extract	or whipping cream

Combine all ingredients until mixture is of proper spreading consistency.

Makes about 1 cup

High Tea Before The Theater
Serves 12

Ham Mousse
Green-on-Green Salad
Savory Duck Pie With Pearl Onions and Madeira Sauce
Grand Marnier Cheese
Nut Crescents
Gewürztraminer
Late Harvest Riesling or Port
Golden Tip Assam Tea

Composing a menu is very much like staging a play. Once the essentials of meal planning are mastered, the menu writer can let the imagination take over. Balance of color and flavors is vital but a dash or two of the unusual brings the audience (your guests) to rapt attention, anticipating each course. Included in this menu are many of the foods typical of British fare (ham, duck, cheese, port, and tea) with interesting twists of presentation and ingredient combinations.

• HAM MOUSSE •

Besides being served on dill bread, as called for here, this mousse can also be served on slices of cucumber. Garnish with a sprig of watercress or a slice of sweet gherkin.

1¼ cups water	2 tablespoons tomato paste
½ cup white wine	1 cup whipping cream, whipped to medium-stiff peaks
2 envelopes unflavored gelatin	
⅓ cup minced onion	2 tablespoons Madeira wine
1 tablespoon butter	1 tablespoon minced parsley
1 cup apple juice	Red leaf lettuce, for accompaniment
1 pound cooked ham, finely chopped	Trumps Dill Bread (see page 52), for accompaniment
2 tablespoons Dijon-style mustard	

1. In a medium bowl combine water, wine, and gelatin; set aside.

2. In a medium skillet sauté onion in butter until limp (3 to 4 minutes). Add apple juice and simmer 2 minutes. Remove from heat and stir in gelatin mixture.

3. In a blender combine half of the gelatin mixture with half of the ham, plus mustard and tomato paste. Blend until smooth. Pour into a large mixing bowl. Repeat for remaining gelatin and ham. Fold in whipped cream, Madeira, and parsley.

4. Pour mixture into an oiled 8-cup mold or 12 oiled individual molds. Chill several hours. Unmold and serve on lettuce leaves with Trumps Dill Bread.

Serves 12

• GREEN-ON-GREEN-SALAD •

Although monochromatic, this sophisticated salad features many shades of green. Chervil has feathery leaves that taste faintly of anise.

3 heads Bibb lettuce, torn into bite-sized pieces	1 teaspoon sugar
	½ teaspoon paprika
1 English cucumber, thinly sliced	¼ teaspoon salt
8 kiwifruit, peeled and sliced	Freshly ground pepper, to taste
¼ cup walnut oil	2 tablespoons minced chervil
¼ cup olive oil	½ cup chopped walnuts or pine nuts, toasted, for garnish
¼ cup fresh lemon juice	

1. Place lettuce on 12 salad plates. Attractively arrange cucumber and kiwifruit slices on lettuce.

2. Combine walnut oil, olive oil, lemon juice, sugar, paprika, salt, pepper, and chervil; mix well. Drizzle over salads, then sprinkle salads with walnuts.

Serves 12

SAVORY DUCK PIE WITH PEARL ONIONS AND MADEIRA SAUCE

Make the Madeira Sauce a day ahead of serving to allow the mushrooms to pick up some of the flavor of the sauce. To serve 12, prepare two pies.

- 2 tablespoons clarified butter
- 1 tablespoon vegetable oil
- 4 duck breast halves, boned and trimmed of excess skin and fat
- ½ teaspoon dried thyme, crushed
- ½ teaspoon dried marjoram, crushed
- 18 to 20 baby pearl onions
- Double Crust Pastry (see below)
- Madeira Sauce (see opposite page)

1. In a large skillet heat clarified butter and oil. Sauté duck breasts over medium heat until brown and crispy on both sides (8 to 10 minutes). Remove with slotted spoon.

2. Combine thyme and marjoram. Roll each duck breast in herbs. Cut breasts into ¼-inch slices; set aside. Boil onions until tender (25 to 30 minutes); set aside.

3. Preheat oven to 425° F. Roll out two thirds of pastry and place in 9-inch pie plate; flute edges. Roll remaining pastry and cut into strips with pastry cutter; set pastry strips aside. Line pastry shell with parchment paper, then add beans or pie weights; bake 5 minutes and remove from oven.

4. Arrange sliced duck breast and pearl onions in pie shell. Pour Madeira Sauce over duck and onions. Arrange pastry strips in a lattice over filling. Bake until pastry is brown (about 25 minutes).

Serves 6

Double Crust Pastry

- 2 cups sifted flour
- 1 teaspoon salt
- ¾ cup vegetable shortening
- 4 to 6 tablespoons chilled water

1. In a large bowl combine flour and salt. Cut in half of the shortening with a pastry blender until mixture is crumbly. Cut in remaining shortening (leave some pieces of shortening the size of lima beans). Add the water, 1 tablespoon at a time, stirring very lightly with a fork.

2. After 4 tablespoons of water have been added, gather dough into a ball and press. If dough will not form a ball and seems dry, add the remaining water, 1 tablespoon at a time. Gather dough into a ball; wrap in plastic and chill for 30 minutes. Use as directed in recipe.

Makes one 9-inch double crust pie crust

Madeira Sauce

- 3 tablespoons dried currants
- ½ cup Cabernet Sauvignon
- 3 cups rich beef stock
- ⅓ cup Madeira
- 2½ tablespoons arrowroot
- ½ pound mushrooms
- 2 tablespoons butter

1. Soak currants in wine 20 minutes. Drain wine into a small saucepan. Reduce wine over medium-high heat to 2 tablespoons (about 8 to 10 minutes). Set aside.

2. In a medium saucepan over medium-high heat, reduce beef stock to 2½ cups (about 10 minutes). Combine Madeira and arrowroot and add to beef stock. Continue cooking until reduced to 2 cups (about 10 minutes). Add reduced red wine from step 1 and currants; set aside.

3. In a large skillet sauté mushrooms in butter until brown and moisture is evaporated (about 2 minutes). Add mushrooms to Madeira mixture. Deglaze skillet with a few tablespoons of Madeira sauce and return drippings to saucepan.

Makes about 3 cups

• GRAND MARNIER CHEESE •

If you prefer not to use the liqueur, substitute 3 tablespoons thawed, undiluted frozen orange juice. Note that the mold must be removed from the refrigerator 1 hour before serving. The recipe can be prepared one day ahead.

- 1 pound Cheddar cheese, shredded
- 6 ounces cream cheese, softened
- 4 to 6 tablespoons Grand Marnier
- 1 teaspoon dry mustard
- Dash cayenne pepper
- 3 apples and 3 pears, cored and sliced, for accompaniment

1. In food processor place cheeses, Grand Marnier, mustard, and cayenne pepper. Process until smooth.

2. Line a 6-cup mold with plastic wrap. Pack cheese in mold. Cover top with plastic wrap. Chill in refrigerator at least 2 hours, or overnight. Remove mold from refrigerator 1 hour before serving.

3. Turn cheese spread out of mold onto large serving board or plate, remove plastic wrap, and surround with sliced apples and pears.

Makes one 6-cup mold, serves 12

• NUT CRESCENTS •

Use vanilla extract with walnuts and almond extract with almonds. Cookies may be rolled in confectioners' sugar rather than dipped in chocolate, if desired. Store cookies airtight for 1 week. Note that the dough must chill 30 minutes before shaping. These elegant cookies would also pair nicely with homemade ice cream or sorbet, or with a cup of espresso.

- 1 cup plus 1 tablespoon butter, softened
- ½ cup sifted confectioners' sugar
- 1 teaspoon vanilla extract or ½ teaspoon almond extract
- 2¼ cups sifted flour
- ¼ teaspoon salt
- ¾ cup finely chopped walnuts or almonds
- 2 ounces semisweet baking chocolate

1. In a medium bowl thoroughly mix 1 cup butter, sugar, and extract. Sift flour and salt together; add to butter-sugar mixture and mix well. Stir in nuts. Wrap dough in plastic wrap and chill 30 minutes.

2. Preheat oven to 400° F. Pinch off balls of dough and roll each into a log. Shape each log into a crescent. Place on ungreased baking sheets. Bake until set but not browned (about 10 minutes); cool on wire racks.

3. In double boiler over simmering water, melt together chocolate and remaining 1 tablespoon butter, stirring constantly. Dip one or both ends of cookie crescents in melted chocolate. Let cookies sit on wire rack to harden.

Makes 3 dozen cookies

TEA DANSANT BUFFET
Serves 24

Champagne

Strawberry-Pineapple-Ginger Punch

Red Cabbage Cups With Roquefort Cheese and Egg Filling

Crudités With Chick-pea Sauce

Cucumber–Cream Cheese Molds

Marinated Beet Salad

Red Potato and Green Bean Salad

Smoked Salmon and Leek Tarts

Stilton Cheesecake

Pavlova

Assorted Cookies and Tarts

Darjeeling Tea

Southern California is known for staging great theme parties. The best caterers specialize in them.

Imagine this: The time is between 4 p.m. and 7 p.m. The lawn is filled with tables bedecked in white linens and the buffet table is covered by a draped white canopy. The dance floor is on the terrace and the orchestra is playing. The women are wearing flowing dresses (ideally, vintage tea dresses); everyone is in the period of the Great Gatsby. The Champagne is flowing.

This is the perfect way to celebrate an engagement or a milestone—a fortieth or fiftieth birthday, perhaps. For a suitable assortment of dessert sweets, consider Orange and Lemon Curd Tarts (see page 78), Viennese Sandwich Cookies (see page 46), and Coconut-Raspberry Madeleines (see page 47).

STRAWBERRY-PINEAPPLE-GINGER PUNCH

Do prepare the Frozen Fruit Ring if you have the time; it adds visual appeal and additional flavor to the punch, and helps to keep it cold.

- 2 packages (10 oz each) frozen strawberries in syrup, thawed
- 8 slices fresh ginger, cut ¼ inch thick
- 1 can (6 oz) frozen pineapple juice concentrate, thawed
- 1 can (6 oz) frozen limeade or lemonade concentrate, thawed
- 3 bottles (1 qt each) ginger ale
- Frozen Fruit Ring (see below), optional

1. In a blender or food processor, purée strawberries and ginger together. Strain to remove seeds and pulp.
2. Combine strawberry-ginger mixture with pineapple juice and limeade concentrates. Pour into punch bowl. Pour in ginger ale and stir to blend. Add Frozen Fruit Ring, if desired.

Makes thirty 4-ounce servings

Frozen Fruit Ring

- 1½ cups pineapple juice
- ½ cup fresh strawberries

Fill a 2-cup ring mold with pineapple juice and strawberries; freeze.

Makes 1 ring

RED CABBAGE CUPS WITH ROQUEFORT CHEESE AND EGG FILLING

Red cabbage makes a pretty color contrast to the pale filling. The cabbage leaves make crispy, edible containers. To serve 24 guests, double the recipe.

- 4 hard-cooked eggs, chopped
- 3 tablespoons crumbled Roquefort cheese
- 3 tablespoons mayonnaise
- ¼ teaspoon hot-pepper sauce
- Salt and freshly ground pepper, to taste
- 1 head red cabbage, leaves separated and trimmed to form 24 cups

Combine eggs, cheese, mayonnaise, and hot-pepper sauce. Taste and season with salt and pepper. Spoon into cabbage-leaf cups.

Serves 12

• CRUDITÉS WITH CHICK-PEA SAUCE •

Assorted fresh vegetables, cut into fancy shapes and spilling out of pretty baskets, are a wonderful presentation and often can be either the focal point of a serving area or a centerpiece on a buffet table. Line the baskets with red leaf lettuce and frilly savoy cabbage. The dipping sauce features chick-peas, also known as garbanzo beans. Tahini is available at Middle Eastern markets.

- 2 bunches carrots, cut into spears
- 2 English cucumbers, sliced with a crinkle chip cutter
- 2 baskets cherry tomatoes
- 1 head cauliflower, blanched, drained, and cut into florets
- 1 bunch broccoli, blanched, drained, and cut into florets
- 2 bunches radishes, cut into roses (see Note, below)
- 2 jicama, cut into ¼-by-2-inch spears
- Chick-pea Sauce (see below)

Prepare vegetables as directed and arrange decoratively. Serve with Chick-pea Sauce for dipping.

Serves 24

Note To make a radish rose, cut 5 petals around radish with a sharp knife; start at top of radish and cut down to within ¼ inch of base. Place radish roses in ice water for several hours and the "petals" will open.

Chick-pea Sauce

- 1 can (15 oz) chick-peas
- ¼ cup fresh lemon juice
- 3 tablespoons tahini (sesame paste)
- 1 to 2 cloves garlic, minced, to taste
- Several drops hot-pepper sauce
- ½ teaspoon salt
- 3 tablespoons water
- Paprika, for garnish

In the bowl of a food processor, place chick-peas, lemon juice, tahini, garlic, hot-pepper sauce, salt, and water. Process until smooth. If sauce seems thick, thin with additional water. Pour sauce into attractive serving dish and sprinkle with paprika.

Makes 1½ cups

Roll back time to the period of the Great Gatsby with a late-afternoon tea dance. On the plate are Salmon and Leek Tart, Crudités, Red Cabbage Cup With Roquefort Cheese and Egg Filling, Marinated Beet Salad, and Red Potato and Green Bean Salad. The dessert is Pavlova. Recipes for Tea Dansant Buffet begin on page 124.

• CUCUMBER–CREAM CHEESE MOLDS •

This cool and refreshing two-layered salad is my favorite. It's practical for entertaining because it can be made one or two days ahead. It also pairs well as a side dish with a main course of cold poached salmon. To serve 24, make a double recipe.

½ envelope unflavored gelatin
1 tablespoon sugar
¼ teaspoon salt
¾ cup boiling water
1 tablespoon fresh lemon juice

⅔ cup thinly sliced, unpared English cucumber
Cucumber–Cream Cheese (see below)
Red leaf lettuce, for garnish

1. In a medium-sized bowl mix together gelatin, sugar, and salt. Add the boiling water to dissolve gelatin, then add lemon juice.

2. Place 3 cucumber slices in bottom of each individual ½-cup mold. (For smaller portions, use miniature muffin tins and line each mold with 1 slice cucumber.) Pour gelatin carefully over cucumber. Chill until firm (about 1 hour).

3. Pour Cucumber–Cream Cheese over gelatin layer. Chill until mixture is firm (8 hours or overnight).

4. Unmold and serve on plates lined with red leaf lettuce.

Makes twelve ½-cup molds

Cucumber–Cream Cheese

1 envelope unflavored gelatin
2 tablespoons sugar
½ teaspoon salt
⅔ cup boiling water
3 tablespoons fresh lemon juice
3 English cucumbers, peeled

8 ounces cream cheese, softened
1 cup mayonnaise
¼ cup chopped onion
¼ cup finely minced parsley
1 teaspoon prepared horseradish

1. In a medium-sized bowl, thoroughly mix together gelatin, sugar, and salt. Add the boiling water to dissolve gelatin, then add lemon juice. Set aside.

2. Cut cucumbers in half lengthwise and remove any seeds. Cut into pieces and place in food processor fitted with metal blade. Process with pulsing motion until coarsely chopped. Place in strainer to drain off excess juice.

3. In bowl of processor place cream cheese, mayonnaise, onion, parsley, and horseradish; blend until combined.

4. Place chopped cucumber in mixing bowl and add cream cheese mixture. Mix well.

Makes about 5 cups

• MARINATED BEET SALAD •

Beet lovers know that this vegetable is very sweet and delicious. Prepare a double recipe to serve 24. Anise seed gives the dressing an unexpected licorice flavor.

- 12 medium beets
- 1½ cups minced onion
- 1 cup mandarin orange sections (optional)
- 1½ cups olive oil
- 1 cup red wine vinegar
- ½ teaspoon salt
- ½ teaspoon cracked black pepper
- 1 tablespoon anise seed, crushed

1. In a large saucepan boil beets until tender (about 35 minutes); let cool.

2. Peel and slice beets. In an attractive serving bowl, combine beets with onion and orange sections (if used).

3. Combine oil, vinegar, salt, pepper, and anise seed. Pour dressing over salad and chill until needed.

Serves 12 as part of a buffet

• RED POTATO AND GREEN BEAN SALAD •

Specialty vegetables are adding a wonderful variety of sizes, shapes, and colors to our tables. Try mixing some of the new blue potatoes with the red-skinned variety called for here. The best selection of this new and exotic harvest will be found at well-stocked produce markets.

- 5 pounds small red new potatoes
- 1 pound green beans, julienned
- ½ cup tarragon vinegar
- ¼ cup sugar
- ½ teaspoon paprika
- Salt and freshly ground pepper, to taste
- ⅓ cup diced green bell pepper
- ⅓ cup diced red bell pepper
- ⅓ cup minced red onion
- 2 teaspoons caraway seed, crushed
- ½ teaspoon celery seed
- 1 cup sour cream
- 1 cup mayonnaise
- Lettuce leaves, for lining bowl

1. In a medium saucepan boil potatoes until just tender (about 20 minutes); let cool and slice ¼ inch thick. Cook julienned beans in 3 inches boiling water until tender-crisp (about 5 minutes). In a large bowl combine cooked potatoes and green beans.

2. Whisk together vinegar, sugar, paprika, salt, and pepper. Marinate potatoes and beans in dressing 1 hour.

3. Gently add bell peppers, red onion, and caraway and celery seed to potato-bean mixture. Combine sour cream and mayonnaise and mix into salad. Cover and refrigerate until well chilled.

4. Line large serving bowl or platter with lettuce. Spoon salad onto lettuce.

Serves 24 as part of a buffet

• SMOKED SALMON AND LEEK TARTS •

To serve this as an entrée, bake filling in a 9-inch pie crust. Leeks are the national symbol of Wales. They tend to be gritty, so be sure to clean them well.

- 1 recipe unbaked Cream Cheese Pastry Shells (see page 37)
- 1 egg, separated, plus 3 whole eggs
- 2 medium or 3 small leeks, trimmed, washed, and sliced
- 1 tablespoon butter
- 6 ounces smoked salmon (lox), chopped
- 1 cup grated Swiss cheese
- 1¼ cups half-and-half
- 1 to 2 tablespoons chopped dill, to taste
- ¼ teaspoon salt
- ¼ teaspoon white pepper
- Dill sprigs, for garnish

1. Brush pastry shells with lightly beaten egg white; set aside. Preheat oven to 425° F.
2. In a medium skillet sauté leeks in butter until limp.
3. Distribute leeks and salmon over bottom of pastry shells and sprinkle with cheese.
4. Combine 3 eggs, the egg yolk, half-and-half, dill, salt, and pepper; whisk to blend. Pour over cheese.
5. Bake tarts 15 minutes. Reduce oven temperature to 350° F and continue baking until top is golden brown (about 15 minutes).
6. Remove from oven and cool 5 to 10 minutes. Garnish with sprigs of dill.

Makes 24 tarts

• STILTON CHEESECAKE •

Stilton is a firm, slightly crumbly, blue-veined English cheese. Traditionally it is served in a large wheel. Here it stars in a savory, sophisticated appetizer cheesecake. It would be delicious served with port.

- 1½ tablespoons butter, melted
- ⅓ cup fine dried bread crumbs
- ¼ cup finely chopped walnuts
- ¼ cup freshly grated Parmesan cheese
- 24 ounces cream cheese
- 8 ounces Stilton cheese
- 4 eggs
- ½ cup whipping cream
- ½ teaspoon salt

1. Preheat oven to 325° F. Grease a 9-inch springform or 8-inch square baking pan with the butter. In a small mixing bowl, combine bread crumbs, walnuts, and Parmesan cheese. Press mixture into bottom and sides of pan; refrigerate.

2. In a large mixing bowl, combine cream cheese and Stilton; mix until smooth. Add eggs, one at a time, mixing well after each addition. Mix in cream and salt.

3. Pour cheese mixture into prepared pan. Bake until set (about 1 hour and 20 minutes). Cool in oven with oven off and door ajar for 1 hour.

Makes 8 to 10 appetizer servings, or 25 squares

• PAVLOVA •

Named in honor of the Russian dancer Anna Pavlova, this special meringue-based dessert is a pretty way to present fresh fruits of the season. New Zealand claims it as its own creation. Prepare 3 recipes for a party of 24 people.

- 4 egg whites
- ¼ teaspoon salt
- 1¼ cups sugar
- 3 tablespoons cold water
- 1 tablespoon cornstarch
- 1 teaspoon vanilla extract
- 1 teaspoon vinegar
- 1 pint raspberries, washed, dried, and hulled
- 2 kiwifruit
- 4 fresh peaches, peeled and sliced ¼ inch thick
- Orange Whipped Cream (see below)

1. Preheat oven to 350° F. Cut a piece of waxed paper to fit bottom of an 8-inch springform pan. Cut a strip wide and long enough to fit around the inside walls of the pan. Line pan with waxed paper and grease well with butter. Sprinkle inside lightly with cold water.

2. In a large bowl of electric mixer, combine egg whites and salt. Beat until soft peaks form. Add sugar gradually and continue beating until sugar is thoroughly incorporated. Add the water and beat well. Beat in cornstarch. Add vanilla and vinegar; beat until egg whites are glossy and stiff peaks form when beater is lifted.

3. Turn meringue into prepared pan and spread evenly. Bake 15 minutes. If meringue has started to rise, turn off heat and let it sit in oven for 1 hour. If it has not started to rise, turn oven down to 250° F and bake another 10 to 15 minutes, then turn off oven and let meringue sit in oven 1 hour. Remove from oven, allow to cool completely, then remove from pan to a serving platter.

4. To serve, top meringue with the fresh fruit and whipped cream.

Serves 8

Orange Whipped Cream

- 1 cup whipping cream
- 2 tablespoons sugar
- 2 tablespoons orange-flavored liqueur

Whip cream; gently fold in sugar and liqueur.

Makes about 2 cups

HOLIDAY DESSERT TEA
Serves 24

Christmas Sparkler

Pumpkin-Mincemeat Bavarian

Marylou's Steamed Carrot Pudding With Brandy Hard Sauce

Cranberry Curd Tarts

Rum, Raisin, and Pecan Pie

Shimmering Cream Cookie Bars

Christmas Lights

Christmas Carol Fruitcakes

Candied Grapefruit Peel

Sugared Nuts

Grandmary's Favorite Caramel Fudge

Formosa Oolong Tea

This tea affair will surely satisfy everyone's sweet tooth. All the recipes can be prepared prior to the day of the party, except for the punch. You will need some time to fill the tart shells with cranberry curd, and time to set up the buffet table. The recipes provide a quantity of food that is realistic for this type of a party; when guests are presented with so many sweets, they tend to take smaller portions than if eating only a single dessert. You may wish to double or triple some of the recipes depending on your guests. Make the fruitcakes at least one month ahead.

Since evening falls early in winter, you can set the stage beginning at the entryway with hurricane lamps. Fill the house with candles and votives, some scented with bayberry. Set baskets of pinecones, pretty bowls of holiday-scented potpourri, and assorted containers filled with nuts in their shells and winter fruits around the house. Ribbon in holiday colors and patterns can be fashioned into bows and tucked here and there, adding further to the festive feeling.

• CHRISTMAS SPARKLER •

Champagne and sparkling wine add sparkle to a pretty, pink-tinted holiday punch. Note that the strawberries and lime juice must chill before blending with the alcohol.

- 1 package (10 oz) frozen strawberries in syrup, thawed
- 2 tablespoons fresh lime juice
- 1 bottle (750 ml) sparkling Burgundy or sparkling white Zinfandel
- 1 bottle (750 ml) Champagne

1. In a blender purée strawberries and lime juice. Strain to remove seeds. Chill.
2. Pour chilled juice into punch bowl. Slowly add Burgundy and Champagne.

Makes fourteen 4-ounce servings

• PUMPKIN-MINCEMEAT BAVARIAN •

Both the gingersnap crust and pumpkin-mincemeat filling are classic holiday flavors. Note that the filling must chill at least 6 hours or overnight. This recipe can be prepared one or two days ahead.

- 2½ cups gingersnap crumbs
- ¼ cup melted butter
- 1 cup milk
- ½ cup firmly packed brown sugar
- 4 eggs, separated
- 2 envelopes unflavored gelatin
- 1 can (16 oz) pumpkin
- 2 teaspoons finely grated orange rind
- 1 teaspoon ground cinnamon
- ¼ teaspoon ground ginger
- ½ teaspoon grated nutmeg
- ¼ teaspoon ground cloves
- 1½ cups whipping cream
- ⅓ cup granulated sugar
- ½ cup mincemeat
- 5 teaspoons dark rum
- 1 tablespoon confectioners' sugar
- Sugared Nuts (see page 138), for garnish

1. Preheat oven to 350° F. Combine gingersnap crumbs and melted butter. Press crumbs onto bottom and 3 inches up sides of a 9-inch springform pan. Bake 6 minutes. Remove and cool.

2. In a 2-quart saucepan combine milk, brown sugar, egg yolks, and gelatin; cook over low heat until mixture thickens (about 7 minutes), stirring constantly. Remove from heat. Blend in pumpkin, orange rind, cinnamon, ginger, nutmeg, and cloves.

3. In a small bowl whip 1 cup of the whipping cream until soft peaks form. Add granulated sugar and continue beating until firmer peaks form. Set aside.

4. In a large mixing bowl, beat egg whites until stiff, but not dry. Fold pumpkin mixture into egg whites, then fold in sweetened cream. Remove 1 cup of the mixture and combine with the mincemeat.

5. Pour half of the pumpkin mixture into crust. Spoon mincemeat mixture on top, then pour in remaining pumpkin mixture; smooth top. Refrigerate for at least 6 hours.

6. To serve beat the remaining ½ cup whipping cream to soft peaks. Add rum and confectioners' sugar and whip until firm peaks form. Pipe whipped cream on top of bavarian and garnish with Sugared Nuts. Remove sides of springform pan and serve.

Serves 10

• MARYLOU'S STEAMED CARROT PUDDING •

Steamed puddings are an English Christmas tradition. Special dome-shaped pudding molds, or basins, are reserved just for holiday use. Well-stocked gourmet cookware stores offer these English molds, as do some mail-order catalogs. This is not as rich as plum pudding and doesn't contain animal fat. The pudding may be made ahead of time and refrigerated up to a week or frozen. Reheat by steaming for 25 minutes.

5 tablespoons flour	1 cup grated raw carrot
1 teaspoon baking soda	1 cup grated raw potato
1 teaspoon ground cinnamon	5 tablespoons firmly packed brown sugar
½ teaspoon grated nutmeg	
½ teaspoon ground cloves	2 tablespoons butter or margarine, melted
½ cup seedless raisins	
½ cup dried currants	Brandy Hard Sauce (see below)

1. Into a mixing bowl sift together flour, baking soda, cinnamon, nutmeg, and cloves. Stir in raisins and currants. Add carrot, potato, brown sugar, and melted butter; mix thoroughly.

2. Pour mixture into greased 1-quart mold. Cover mold with waxed paper and tie securely, then cover with mold lid or with aluminum foil.

3. Place mold on a rack over simmering water and steam 3 hours. Unmold onto platter and serve with Brandy Hard Sauce.

Serves 6 to 8

Brandy Hard Sauce

½ cup butter, softened	2 tablespoons brandy
1¼ cups sifted confectioners' sugar	½ teaspoon grated nutmeg
½ teaspoon vanilla extract	

Beat butter until fluffy. Add confectioners' sugar, vanilla, and brandy; mix thoroughly. Place in an attractive serving dish and sprinkle with nutmeg.

Makes 1½ cups

• CRANBERRY CURD TARTS •

Aside from serving as a tart filling, cranberry curd may also be used to spread on scones or as a filling for butter cakes. It will keep for up to 2 weeks in the refrigerator.

- 3½ cups (12 oz) fresh cranberries
- 1 cup sugar
- 5 large egg yolks
- 1½ tablespoons fresh lemon juice
- ½ cup unsalted butter, melted
- 2 tablespoons kirsch or cranberry liqueur
- 1 recipe baked Cream Cheese Pastry Shells (see page 37)

1. In medium saucepan cook cranberries with ½ cup of the sugar over low heat until they are soft (12 to 15 minutes). Stir occasionally to prevent scorching.

2. In a blender or food processor, purée cooked cranberries until smooth. Press through a fine sieve to remove seeds.

3. In a double boiler combine cranberry purée, egg yolks, remaining ½ cup sugar, lemon juice, and melted butter. Cook over simmering water until thick (about 10 minutes), stirring occasionally.

4. Cool and add kirsch. Refrigerate, tightly covered, until needed. To serve fill prepared pastry shells with curd.

Makes 24 miniature tarts

• RUM, RAISIN, AND PECAN PIE •

This pie is great for a Thanksgiving or Christmas feast. It also travels well. I have taken it with me when we visit my husband's family—a drive of about 400 miles. The pie can be reheated in a 325° F oven for about 10 minutes.

- 1½ cups sugar
- 1 cup raisins
- ¾ cup half-and-half
- ½ cup unsalted butter
- 6 egg yolks
- 1½ cups coarsely chopped pecans
- 2 tablespoons dark rum
- 1 tablespoon fresh lemon juice
- ½ tablespoon vanilla extract
- ¼ teaspoon salt
- 1 recipe unbaked Single Crust Pastry (see page 26)

1. In a medium saucepan combine sugar, raisins, half-and-half, and butter; bring to a boil. Reduce heat to low and simmer 2 minutes, stirring frequently. Remove from heat and cool slightly.

2. Preheat oven to 425° F. In a large bowl beat egg yolks lightly, then beat in hot sugar mixture. Stir in pecans, rum, lemon juice, vanilla, and salt.

3. Pour filling into pie shell. Bake 15 minutes, then reduce temperature to 375° F and continue baking until puffed and golden (40 to 45 minutes). Remove from oven and cool 30 minutes to 1 hour.

Serves 6 to 8

• SHIMMERING CREAM COOKIE BARS •

A perfect afternoon tea treat, these tiny cookie bars are especially pretty for the Christmas holidays or for Valentine's Day. Two recipes can be prepared; use lime gelatin for the topping of the second recipe and you will have a combination of both red and green Shimmering Cream Cookie Bars. The bars can be prepared one or two days prior to serving; any leftover bars will keep several days in the refrigerator.

- ¾ cup butter
- ½ cup firmly packed brown sugar
- 1½ cups flour
- 1 cup chopped walnuts
- 1 package (3 oz) lemon gelatin
- 4 cups hot water
- ½ cup sugar
- 8 ounces cream cheese
- 1 carton (9 oz) prepared dessert topping
- 1 package (6 oz) strawberry, raspberry, or cherry gelatin

1. Preheat oven to 350° F. In a medium bowl cream together butter and brown sugar. Add flour and walnuts, then mix (mixture will be crumbly). Press mixture into lightly greased 9- by 13-inch pan and bake until top is lightly browned (about 10 minutes); cool on a wire rack.

2. Dissolve lemon gelatin in 1 cup of the hot water. Cool.

3. Blend sugar and cream cheese together. Add dessert topping. Combine with cooled gelatin. Pour mixture over baked crust and chill until firm, about 4 hours.

4. Dissolve strawberry, raspberry, or cherry gelatin in the remaining 3 cups hot water; cool slightly. Pour over top of cheese mixture. Chill until firm.

5. Cut into bite-sized bars and serve in paper bonbon cups.

Makes 4 to 6 dozen bars

• CHRISTMAS LIGHTS •

The sugar crystals on the gumdrops that are mixed into the batter cause these cookies to sparkle like the lights on a Christmas tree. If stored airtight, these bars will keep for up to four or five days.

- 4 eggs
- 2 cups sugar
- 3 tablespoons butter, melted and cooled
- 2 cups cake flour
- ¼ teaspoon salt
- 2 teaspoons vanilla extract
- 1½ cups toasted slivered almonds
- 1½ cups small gumdrops (use red and green ones)

1. Preheat oven to 325° F. Grease and flour a 9- by 13-inch glass baking dish; set aside. Using an electric mixer beat eggs until very light. Gradually add sugar, beating all the time. Mixture should be thick and light-colored. Add melted butter.

2. Into a large bowl sift flour with salt; add to egg mixture. Stir in vanilla, almonds, and gumdrops.

3. Spread batter into baking dish. Bake 30 minutes; cool slightly and cut into bars.

Makes 24 bars

• CHRISTMAS CAROL FRUITCAKES •

To allow the cakes to age and properly absorb the brandy, the fruitcakes must be made 4 to 6 weeks before you need them. I usually bake mine in early November. The fruitcake batter can be baked in whatever size pans suit your needs. I usually get eight 3- by 5-inch loaves and about 60 bonbon-sized miniature cakes from this amount of batter.

- ½ cup dry sherry
- 2 pounds golden raisins
- 3 pounds dates, pitted and quartered, or 2 pounds dates and 1 pound dried currants
- 1½ pounds candied cherries, halved
- 1½ pounds candied pineapple wedges
- ½ pound candied apricots
- ½ pound diced candied orange peel
- ½ pound diced candied lemon peel
- 1½ pounds walnut halves
- 1½ pounds pecan halves
- 3½ cups flour
- 1 cup plus 2 tablespoons butter, softened
- 3½ cups sugar
- 7 eggs, at room temperature
- 1½ teaspoons baking soda
- 1 teaspoon ground cinnamon
- ½ teaspoon grated nutmeg
- ½ teaspoon ground mace
- ½ teaspoon ground cloves
- ½ teaspoon ground allspice
- 1 tablespoon vanilla extract
- ⅓ cup bourbon
- 1 cup plus 2 tablespoons white wine
- ⅓ cup orange-flavored liqueur
- 1 tablespoon grated orange rind
- 1 tablespoon grated lemon rind
- Brandy, for soaking (to taste)
- Fruitcake Glaze (see opposite page)
- Additional candied fruits, for decorating tops of fruitcakes

1. Line 3- by 5-inch loaf pans first with heavy brown paper (grease the paper), then with greased waxed paper. (If using miniature paper cups, put a few drops vegetable oil on each paper, and place in miniature muffin tins.)

2. Pour sherry into a large bowl. Add the raisins and dates. Allow these fruits to plump for 12 hours. Stir occasionally.

3. Preheat oven to 250°F. Add candied fruit and nuts to the raisin-date mixture. Add 1 cup of the flour and mix until fruits and nuts are evenly coated. Set aside.

4. In a large bowl cream butter and sugar. Add the eggs, one at a time, beating well after each addition.

5. Into a large bowl sift together the remaining 2½ cups flour, baking soda, cinnamon, nutmeg, mace, cloves, and allspice. Add vanilla, bourbon, wine, liqueur, and citrus rinds; mix well. Mix into creamed butter-sugar-egg mixture. Pour the batter over the fruit-nut mixture, and mix thoroughly.

6. Spoon fruitcake batter into prepared loaf pans, filling to within ¼ inch of top.

7. Place a small pan of water on the lowest rack of the oven. Bake loaves until an inserted toothpick comes out clean (about 2½ hours). Check pan of water after an hour and replenish if needed. Miniature fruitcakes will take about 45 minutes.

8. Allow fruitcakes to cool in pans on a rack. Loosen and turn out. Remove brown and waxed papers. Wrap cakes in plastic wrap and aluminum foil. Replace cakes in baking pans if using gift foil pans.

9. Each week for several weeks, unwrap the fruitcakes and spoon a tablespoon of brandy over the tops. After 4 to 6 weeks, unwrap cakes and place them on a wire rack. Brush tops with hot glaze, decorate with candied fruits, and brush with additional glaze. Allow glaze to harden, then gift wrap.

Makes about 12 pounds fruitcake

Fruitcake Glaze

½ cup sugar	1 cup juice from canned fruit

In a small saucepan, heat sugar and fruit juice until sugar is dissolved.

Makes about 1 cup

• CANDIED GRAPEFRUIT PEEL •

My mother had two grapefruit trees; one she always referred to as her "candy" tree. Note that making candied peel is a two-day process. If stored in an airtight container, candied peel will keep for several months.

3 large grapefruit	1 cup water
1 tablespoon salt	Red or green food coloring
1 cup sugar, plus sugar for coating	(optional)

1. Remove peel from grapefruit in several sections. With a sharp knife remove most of white membrane, leaving the peel about ⅛ inch thick.

2. Soak peel overnight in 1 quart cold water mixed with 1 tablespoon salt. Drain, cover with cold water, bring to the boiling point, and boil 20 minutes. Repeat three times and cook in the last water until tender (about 2 hours); check peel every half hour with the tip of a sharp knife. Drain and let cool.

3. Cut peel into strips about ¼ inch wide. In a heavy-bottomed pan combine 1 cup sugar and water. Bring to a boil and add prepared peel. Cook slowly until the peel is almost transparent (35 minutes to 1 hour, depending on degree of transparency desired); watch mixture as it cooks so that it doesn't scorch. Add food coloring if desired.

4. Remove peel with a skimmer and spread on a plate to cool. Roll peel in sugar and spread on waxed paper to dry.

Makes about 1 pound, 2 cups

Chocolate-Dipped Peel

Instead of rolling peel in sugar, dip in 2 ounces melted semisweet chocolate. Place on waxed paper to set.

• SUGARED NUTS •

These make delicious and much-appreciated gifts. Look for colorful tins or baskets to pack them in for presentation. Stored airtight, the nuts will keep 2 to 3 weeks.

- 1 cup firmly packed brown sugar
- 1 teaspoon ground cinnamon
- 4 tablespoons water
- Pinch cream of tartar
- 3 cups walnut halves

1. In a 2-quart saucepan combine sugar and cinnamon. Stir in the water and cream of tartar. Cook until mixture reaches the soft-ball stage (230° F on a candy thermometer).

2. Remove from heat and immediately stir in walnuts until all are coated. Spread onto a thin layer of waxed paper or a buttered plate. When cool, separate into small pieces.

Makes 3 cups nuts

• GRANDMARY'S FAVORITE • CARAMEL FUDGE

My mother's name was Mary and my children called her Grandmary. We always presented Grandmary with a box of this fudge for Christmas or on her birthday. It is also my son's favorite and must be hidden away so it doesn't disappear before the guests arrive. For a party serve squares in decorative paper cups.

- 2 tablespoons butter
- ⅔ cup undiluted evaporated milk
- 1⅔ cups sugar
- ½ teaspoon salt
- 1½ cups miniature marshmallows
- 1½ cups butterscotch chips
- 1 teaspoon vanilla extract
- ½ cup chocolate chips
- ½ cup chopped walnuts

1. In a 2-quart saucepan combine butter, evaporated milk, sugar, and salt; bring to a boil over medium heat. Cook 5 minutes, stirring constantly (start timing when mixture starts to bubble around the edges of pan).

2. Remove from heat. Stir in marshmallows, butterscotch chips, and vanilla. Stir vigorously until all marshmallows are melted and mixture is smooth. Pour into greased 9-inch square pan and cool.

3. Melt chocolate chips in double boiler over hot water. Spread melted chocolate over fudge. Sprinkle with chopped nuts. Allow to set, then cut into squares.

Makes 36 pieces

Where to Enjoy Afternoon Tea

Atlanta
The Ritz Carlton Downtown
The Ritz Carlton Buckhead

Boston
The Ritz Carlton

Chicago
The Drake
The Ritz Carlton
Park Hyatt

Dallas
The Adolphus Hotel
The Mansion on Turtle Creek

Denver
The Brown Palace Hotel

London
Harrod's
The Ritz

Los Angeles
The Sheraton Grande
Trumps

New York
The Plaza
The Waldorf Astoria

Philadelphia
The Four Seasons Hotel

San Francisco
The Stanford Court

Victoria, British Columbia
The Empress

U.S. Measure and Metric Measure Conversion Chart

Formulas for Exact Measures

Measure	Symbol	When You Know	Multiply by	To Find
Mass (weight)	oz	ounces	28.35	grams
	lb	pounds	0.45	kilograms
	g	grams	0.035	ounces
	kg	kilograms	2.2	pounds
Volume	tsp	teaspoons	4.9	milliliters
	tbsp	tablespoons	15.0	milliliters
	fl oz	fluid ounces	29.57	milliliters
	c	cups	0.237	liters
	pt	pints	0.47	liters
	qt	quarts	0.95	liters
	gal	gallons	3.785	liters
	ml	milliliters	0.034	fluid ounces
Temperature	° F	Fahrenheit	5/9 (after subtracting 32)	Celsius
	° C	Celsius	9/5 (then add 32)	Fahrenheit

Rounded Measures for Quick Reference

Mass (weight)	1 oz		= 30 g
	4 oz		= 115 g
	8 oz		= 225 g
	16 oz	= 1 lb	= 450 g
	32 oz	= 2 lb	= 900 g
	36 oz	= 2¼ lb	= 1,000 g (1 kg)
Volume	¼ tsp	= 1/24 oz	= 1 ml
	½ tsp	= 1/12 oz	= 2 ml
	1 tsp	= 1/6 oz	= 5 ml
	1 tbsp	= ½ oz	= 15 ml
	1 c	= 8 oz	= 250 ml
	2 c (1 pt)	= 16 oz	= 500 ml
	4 c (1 qt)	= 32 oz	= 1 liter
	4 qt (1 gal)	= 128 oz	= 3¾ liter
Temperature	32° F	= 0° C	
	68° F	= 20° C	
	212° F	= 100° C	

INDEX

Note: Page numbers in italics refer to photographs separated from recipe text.

A
Afternoon tea, 9, 18, 103–111
  hotels serving, 139
  planning, 14–15
Apples
  Apple-Ginger Marmalade, *34,* 38
  Ham, Cabbage, Gruyère, and Apple Salad, 104
  Waldorf Salad Supreme, 113
Apricot Glaze, 39
Apricot Mist Punch, *66,* 68
Artichoke Dip, 86, *91*
Asparagus Rolls, 44
Avocado
  Avocado-Bacon Spread, 19
  Mini-Tortillas With Guacamole and Shrimp, 98
  Tender Greens Tossed With Cantaloupe and, *74,* 76

B
Banana Spears Dipped in Chocolate, Coconut, and Peanuts, 116
Beverages
  Apricot Mist Punch, *66,* 68
  Christmas Sparkler, 132
  Frozen Fruit Ring for, 124
  Lemon Mint Spritzers, 60
  Olallieberry Champagne Kir, 25
  Raspberry Champagne Punch, 49
  Rhubarb Punch, 98
  Strawberry-Pineapple-Ginger Punch, 124
Bouchées With Smoked Oyster Pâté, *66,* 68–69
Breads
  Chocolate Date-Nut, 44
  Lemon, 72
  Mini-Tortillas With Guacamole and Shrimp, 98
  Peanut Butter, 50
  Pineapple, 52
  special presentations, 22–23
  Strawberry-Pecan, 73
  Trumps Dill, 52
Brewing tea, 15
Brie, Baked, With Roasted Garlic, *30,* 31
Brunch. *See* Elevenses
Butters. *See* Spreads

C
Cabbage
  Colcannon, 94
  Ham, Cabbage, Gruyère, and Apple Salad, 104
  Red Cabbage Cups With Roquefort Cheese and Egg Filling, 124, *126*
Cakes
  See also Cheesecake; Fruitcake
  Chocolate Marmalade, *106–7,* 109
  Gingerbread, 89
  Lemon Pound, 108
  Orange-Glazed Oatmeal, 28
  Southern Bourbon, *30,* 33
Candies
  Candied Grapefruit Peel, 137
  Chocolate-Dipped Peel, 137
  Grandmary's Favorite Caramel Fudge, 138
Carrots
  Cream of Tomato and Carrot Soup With Fennel, 81
  Marylou's Steamed Carrot Pudding, 133
Caviar, Zesty Deviled Eggs With, *66,* 71
Celery Stuffed With Pimiento-Olive Cream Cheese, 113
Charlotte, Lemon Raspberry, 54–55
Cheese
  See also Cheesecake
  Baked Brie With Roasted Garlic, *30,* 31
  Celery Stuffed With Pimiento-Olive Cream Cheese, 113
  Cheese Wafers, 36
  Chèvre Tart, 26
  Chutney Cream Cheese, 19
  Coeur à la Crème With Berries, *42–43,* 45
  Cucumber–Cream Cheese Molds, 127
  Fresh Beet, Belgian Endive, and Gruyère Salad, 82
  Grand Marnier, 121
  Ham, Cabbage, Gruyère, and Apple Salad, 104
  Herbed Coeur à la Crème, 104
  Pear, Gorgonzola, and Toasted Pecan Salad, 87, *91*

Cheese *(continued)*
  Potted Shrimp, 93
  Red Cabbage Cups With Roquefort Cheese and Egg Filling, 124, *126*
  Smoked Salmon Spread, 41
Cheesecake
  Chocolate-Raspberry Truffle, 84
  Stilton, 129
Chick-pea Sauce, 125
Chutney. *See* Condiments
Chutney Cream Cheese, 19
Cinnamon Pastry Spirals, *51,* 54
Coeur à la Crème
  Herbed, 104
  With Berries, *42–43,* 45
Colcannon, 94
Condiments
  Corn Relish, 32
  Cranberry Chutney, 95
  Port Onion Nibbles, 95
  Spicy Melon Relish, *74,* 77
  Szechuan Pepper Salt, 63
  Tomato-Mint Chutney, 83
Cookies
  Chocolate Tulip Cookie Cups, 102
  Christmas Lights, 135
  Coconut-Raspberry Madeleines, 47
  Grannie's Shortbread, 38
  Jalapeño Jelly Thumbprint, *74,* 79
  Ladyfingers, 55
  Nut Crescents, 122
  Shimmering Cream Cookie Bars, 135
  Teddy Bear Gingies, *114–15,* 117
  Viennese Sandwich, *42–43,* 46
Cranberry Chutney, 95
Cranberry Curd Tarts, 134
Cranberry Pudding With Bourbon Custard Sauce, *106–7,* 110
Cream, Mock Devonshire, 37
Cream cheese. *See* Cheese; Cheesecake
Cream Puffs, 50
Cream tea, 9, 35–39
Crème Anglaise, Peach, 108
Cucumber–Cream Cheese Molds, 127
Cucumber Hearts, 41
Curd tarts
  Cranberry, 134
  Orange and Lemon, *74,* 78–79
Custard. *See* Crème Anglaise; Puddings

D, E

Date-Nut Bread, Chocolate, 44
Desserts
   See also Cakes; Fruits; Pies; Puddings; Tarts
   Chocolate Truffle Fruit Tarts, 39
   Fresh Peach Trifle, *106–7,* 108
   Lemon Raspberry Charlotte, 54–55
   Pavlova, *126,* 130
   Pumpkin-Mincemeat Bavarian, 132
   Zesty Bosc Pears and Gingered Plum Sorbet in Mandarin Cups, 64
Devonshire Cream, Mock, 37
Dipping sauces
   Artichoke Dip, 86, *91*
   Chick-pea Sauce, 125
   Creamy Mint Sauce, 68
   Hot and Spicy Sesame Sauce, 62
   Mustard Mayonnaise, 89
   Tuscan Garlic Sauce, 89
   Vietnamese, 63
Dumplings, Shao Mai, 62
Egg Filling, Red Cabbage Cups With Roquefort Cheese and, 124, *126*
Egg-Olive Filling, 20
Egg Rolls With Vietnamese Dipping Sauce, 63
Eggs, Zesty Deviled, With Caviar, *66,* 71
Elevenses, 9, 24–28
Endive
   Endive Spears With Duck Liver and Forest Mushroom Pâté, 49
   Fresh Beet, Belgian Endive, and Gruyère Salad, 82
Equipment, 16–17

F

Fillings
   See also Spreads
   Cream Cheese, 44
   Egg-Olive, 20
   Ham Salad, 20
   Peanut Butter, 20
   Potted Shrimp, 93
   Shrimp, 21
Filo pastry
   Pear Picadillo in Filo Baskets, 99
   Tiropitas, *66,* 70

Fish and shellfish
   See also Salmon
   Crab Cakes With Cilantro-Cayenne Mayonnaise, 88, *91*
   Crab and Sun-Dried Tomato Tarts, 69
   Grilled Swordfish With Fresh Tomato-Mint Chutney, 82–83
   Mini-Tortillas With Guacamole and Shrimp, 98
   Papaya Stuffed With Crab Salad, 58, *59*
   Potted Shrimp With Water Biscuits, 93
   Shao Mai Dumplings, 62
   Shrimp Filling, 21
   Smoked Oyster Pâté, *66,* 69
   Southwestern Paella, 25
Fritters, Spicy Vegetable, 88–89, *91*
Frosting
   Chocolate, 46
   Confectioners' Sugar, 117
Fruitcake
   Christmas Carol, 136–37
   Dundee Cake, 96
Fruits
   See also Desserts; *specific fruits*
   Fresh Fruit in Chocolate Tulip Cookie Cups, 102
   Frozen Fruit Ring, 124
   Jicama, Mandarin Orange, and Green Bean Salad, 100
   Prosciutto-Wrapped Fig or Pear Slices, *66,* 72
   Tropical Fruit Salad With Mango Sauce, 27
Fudge, Grandmary's Favorite Caramel, 138

G

Garlic
   Baked Brie With Roasted, *30,* 31
   Tuscan Garlic Sauce, 89
Gingerbread, 89
Glazes
   Apricot, 39
   Fruitcake, 137
   Marmalade, 109
   Orange, 28
   Strawberry, 39
Grand Marnier Cheese, 121
Grapefruit Peel, Candied, 137
Green beans
   Jicama, Mandarin Orange, and Green Bean Salad, 100
   Red Potato and Green Bean Salad, *126,* 128

Guacamole and Shrimp, Mini-Tortillas With, 98

H

Ham
   on Asparagus Rolls, 44
   Ham, Cabbage, Gruyère, and Apple Salad, 104
   Ham and Cheese Roll-Ups, 113
   Ham Mousse, 119
   Ham Salad Filling, 20
   Prosciutto-Wrapped Fig or Pear Slices, *66,* 72
Ham tea, 9
Herb Butter, 20
Herbed Coeur à la Crème, 104
High tea, 9, 18. *See also* Menus

K, L

Kiwifruit
   Frangipane Tartlets, *59,* 60
   Green-on-Green Salad, 119
   in Pavlova, *126,* 130
   Tropical Fruit Salad With Mango Sauce, 27
Ladyfingers, 55
Leeks
   Smoked Salmon and Leek Tarts, *126,* 129
   Sugar Snap Peas With, 101
Lemon Bread, 72
Lemon Curd Tarts, *74,* 78–79
Lemon Mint Spritzers, 60
Lemon Pound Cake, 108
Lemon Raspberry Charlotte, 54–55

M

Madeleines, Coconut-Raspberry, 47
Mango Sauce, Tropical Fruit Salad With, 27
Marmalade, Apple-Ginger, *34,* 38
Marmalade Glaze, 109
Mayonnaise. *See* Spreads
Meats and poultry
   Beef Steak and Kidney Pie, 94
   Chicken Posole, *74,* 76–77
   Chinese Chicken Salad, 64
   Endive Spears With Duck Liver and Forest Mushroom Pâté, 49
   Lamb Vegetable Pasties, 105
   Pear Picadillo in Filo Baskets, 99
   Savory Duck Pie With Pearl Onions and Madeira Sauce, 120–21
   Shao Mai Dumplings, 62

Meats and poultry *(continued)*
  Southwestern Paella, 25
  Tearoom Chicken Salad, 53
  Turkey, Jicama, and Bell Pepper Salad, 87, *91*
  Veal Terrine With Mustard Sauce, 57
Menus
  Afternoon Wedding Reception, 67–73
  Autumn High Tea, 29–33
  Bridal Shower, 48–55
  A Collector's High Tea, 97–102
  Elevenses, 24–28
  formal afternoon tea, 14–15
  Grazing on Melrose, 80–84
  High Tea With Asian Flavors, 61–65
  Holiday Dessert Tea, 131–38
  informal fruit and cheese spread, 18
  May Day Picnic, 56–60
  Nibbling Around Nob Hill, 85–90
  Southwestern Jalapeño High Tea, 75–79
  Tea Dansant Buffet, 123–30
  Tea at Three, 103–111
  Teddy Bear Tea, 112–17
  Valentine's Day Tea, 40–47
  A Very British Farm Tea, 92–96
  Winter Cream Tea, 35–39
Mock Devonshire Cream, 37
Mousse
  Ham, 119
  Salmon, *66*, 71
Muffins
  Blueberry Whole Wheat, 27
  Jalapeño–Blue Cornmeal, *74*, 78
Mushrooms
  Duck Liver and Forest Mushroom Pâté, 49
  in Madeira Sauce, 121
  Mushroom, Pea, and Wild Rice Salad, 86, *91*
  Mushroom Tarts, 36–37
  in Salmon Fillets With Wild Rice Dressing, 100–1
  in Shao Mai Dumplings, 62

N, O
Nursery tea, 12, 112–17
Nuts. *See* Pecans; Walnuts
Olives, Egg-Olive Filling, 20
Onions, Port Onion Nibbles, 95
Orange Curd Tarts, *74*, 78–79
Orange Oatmeal Scones, 58
Orange Whipped Cream, 130

P
Paella, Southwestern, 25
Papaya
  Papaya Stuffed With Crab Salad, 58, *59*
  Tropical Fruit Salad With Mango Sauce, 27
Pasties, Lamb Vegetable, 105
Pastry
  See also Filo pastry
  Bouchées, *66*, 68–69
  Cream Cheese Pastry Shells, 36–37
  Double Crust, 120
  Pâte Brisée, 90
  Single Crust, 26
Pâtés and terrines
  Duck Liver and Forest Mushroom, 49
  Smoked Oyster, *66*, 69
  Veal Terrine With Mustard Sauce, 57
Peaches
  in Pavlova, *126*, 130
  Peach Trifle, *106–7*, 108
Peanut Butter Bread, 50
Peanut Butter Filling, 20
Pears
  Pear, Gorgonzola, and Toasted Pecan Salad, 87, *91*
  Pear Picadillo in Filo Baskets, 99
  Prosciutto-Wrapped Fig or Pear Slices, *66*, 72
  Zesty Bosc, 65
Peas, Mushroom, Pea, and Wild Rice Salad, 86, *91*
Pecans
  Chocolate Date-Nut Bread, 44
  Pear, Gorgonzola, and Toasted Pecan Salad, 87, *91*
  Pecan Butter, 21
  Rum, Raisin, and Pecan Pie, 134
  Strawberry-Pecan Bread, 73
  Viennese Sandwich Cookies, *42–43*, 46
Pies
  Beef Steak and Kidney, 94
  Rum, Raisin, and Pecan, 134
  Savory Duck, With Pearl Onions and Madeira Sauce, 120–21
Pineapple Bread, 52
Planning a formal tea, 14–15
Plum Sorbet, Gingered, 64
Potatoes
  Colcannon, 94
  Red Potato and Green Bean Salad, *126*, 128
Poultry. *See* Meats and poultry

Prosciutto-Wrapped Fig or Pear Slices, *66*, 72
Puddings
  Baked Custard, 53
  Cranberry Pudding With Bourbon Custard Sauce, *106–7*, 110
  Marylou's Steamed Carrot, 133
  Pumpkin-Mincemeat Bavarian, 132

R
Raspberries
  Chocolate-Raspberry Truffle Cheesecake, 84
  Coconut-Raspberry Madeleines, 47
  Lemon Raspberry Charlotte, 54–55
  in Pavlova, *126*, 130
  Raspberry Butter, 21
  Raspberry Champagne Punch, 49
  Raspberry Sauce, 45
  Raspberry Whipped Cream, 55
Relish
  Corn, 32
  Spicy Melon, *74*, 77
  Tomato-Mint Chutney, 83
Rhubarb Punch, 98
Rice
  Mushroom, Pea, and Wild Rice Salad, 86, *91*
  Salmon Fillets With Wild Rice Dressing, 100–1
  Southwestern Paella, 25
  Wild Rice Pilaf in Pasilla Chiles, 83
Rolls, Cinnamon Pastry Spirals, *51*, 54

S
Salad dressings
  French Vinaigrette, 93
  Honey-Lime, 53
  Jalapeño-Soy, 87, *91*
  Minted Orange-Walnut Vinaigrette, 100
  Mustard-Herb Vinaigrette, 86
  Orange-Walnut Vinaigrette, 82
  Sesame Dressing, 64
  Tarragon Vinaigrette, 76
Salads
  Chicken
  Chinese Chicken, 64
  Cucumber–Cream Cheese Molds, 127
  Fresh Beet, Belgian Endive, and Gruyère, 82
  Green-on-Green, 119

Salads *(continued)*
    Ham, Cabbage, Gruyère, and Apple, 104
    Jicama, Mandarin Orange, and Green Bean, 100
    Marinated Beet, *126,* 128
    Mushroom, Pea, and Wild Rice, 86, *91*
    Papaya Stuffed With Crab Salad, 58, *59*
    Pear, Gorgonzola, and Toasted Pecan, 87, *91*
    Red Potato and Green Bean, *126,* 128
    Tender Greens Tossed With Cantaloupe and Avocado, *74,* 76
    Turkey, Jicama, and Bell Pepper, 87, *91*
    Waldorf Salad Supreme, 113
    Watercress Sprigs With French Vinaigrette, 93
    Weyburn Salad Plate, *51,* 53
Salmon
    Salmon Fillets With Wild Rice Dressing, 100–1
    Salmon Mousse, *66,* 71
    Smoked Salmon Hearts, 41
    Smoked Salmon and Leek Tarts, *126,* 129
Salt, Szechuan Pepper, 63
Sandwiches, 18–23
    See also Fillings
    Asparagus Rolls, 44
    Cucumber Hearts, 41
    Ham and Cheese Roll-Ups, 113
    Smoked Salmon Hearts, 41
    special presentations for, 22–23
    Watercress, 57, *59*
Sauces
    See also Dipping sauces
    Bourbon Custard, 110
    Brandy Hard, 133
    Chardonnay Tarragon, 101
    Chick-pea, 125
    Creamy Mint, 68
    Hot and Spicy Sesame Sauce, 62
    Madeira, 121
    Mango, 27
    Raspberry, 45
    Spicy-Sweet Mustard, 96
Scones
    Calico Cornmeal, 32
    Currant, *34,* 37
    Orange Oatmeal, 58
Shellfish. *See* Fish and shellfish

Shortbread, Grannie's, 38
Sorbet, Gingered Plum, 64
Soups
    Acorn Squash Bisque, *30,* 31
    Cream of Tomato and Carrot Soup With Fennel, 81
Spreads
    See also Fillings; Pâtés and terrines
    Apple-Ginger Marmalade, *34,* 38
    Avocado-Bacon Spread, 19
    Basil-Parmesan Mayonnaise, 19
    Chutney Cream Cheese, 19
    Cilantro-Cayenne Mayonnaise, 88, *91*
    Dill-Mint Mayonnaise, 20
    Herb Butter, 20
    Mustard Mayonnaise, 89
    Pecan Butter, 21
    Raspberry Butter, 21
    Smoked Salmon Spread, 41
    Spicy-Sweet Mustard Sauce, 96
    Tomato Butter, 21
    Watercress Mayonnaise, 21
Strawberries
    Chocolate-Dipped, *106–7,* 111
    in Christmas Sparkler, 132
    Coeur à la Crème With Berries, *42–43,* 45
    Frangipane Tartlets, *59,* 60
    Strawberry Glaze, 39
    Strawberry-Pecan Bread, 73
    Strawberry-Pineapple-Ginger Punch, 124
Strawberry tea, 12
Sugar Snap Peas With Leeks, 101
Summer tea, 12
Szechuan Pepper Salt, 63

T
Table settings, 15, 16–18
Tarts
    Bouchées With Smoked Oyster Pâté, *66,* 68–69
    Chèvre, 26
    Chocolate Truffle Fruit, 39
    Crab and Sun-Dried Tomato, 69
    Cranberry Curd, 134
    Cream Puffs With Ham Salad Filling and Shrimp Filling, 70
    Frangipane Tartlets, *59,* 60
    Lemon-Almond Chess, 90
    Mushroom, 36–37
    Orange and Lemon Curd, *74,* 78–79
    Smoked Salmon and Leek, *126,* 129

Teas, 12–15. *See also* Menus
Tea sandwiches. *See* Sandwiches
Techniques
    brewing tea, 15
    handling chiles, 83
    making a radish rose, 125
    special presentations, 22–23
Terrines. *See* Pâtés and terrines
Tomatoes
    Crab and Sun-Dried Tomato Tarts, 69
    Cream of Tomato and Carrot Soup With Fennel, 81
    Tomato Butter, 21
    Tomato-Mint Chutney, 83
Tortillas, Mini-Tortillas With Guacamole and Shrimp, 98
Trifle, Fresh Peach, *106–7,* 108

V
Vegetables
    See also Salads; *specific vegetables*
    Crudités With Chick-pea Sauce, 125
    Spicy Vegetable Fritters, 88–89, *91*

W
Walnuts
    Minted Orange-Walnut Vinaigrette, 100
    Nut Crescents, 122
    Orange-Walnut Vinaigrette, 82
    Sugared Nuts, 138
Watercress
    Tender Greens Tossed With Cantaloupe and Avocado, *74,* 76
    Watercress Mayonnaise, 21
    Watercress Sandwiches, 57, *59*
    Watercress Sprigs With French Vinaigrette, 93
Whipped cream
    in Mock Devonshire Cream, 37
    Orange, 130
    Raspberry, 55
Wild rice. *See* Rice
Winter tea, 12, 35–39